Theatre
in
Dachau

Rev. Hermanus Knoop (left) and Rev. Klaas Schilder, ca. 1930, when both of them were ministers of the Reformed (*Gereformeerd*) Church of Rotterdam-Delfshaven.

A
Theatre
in
Dachau

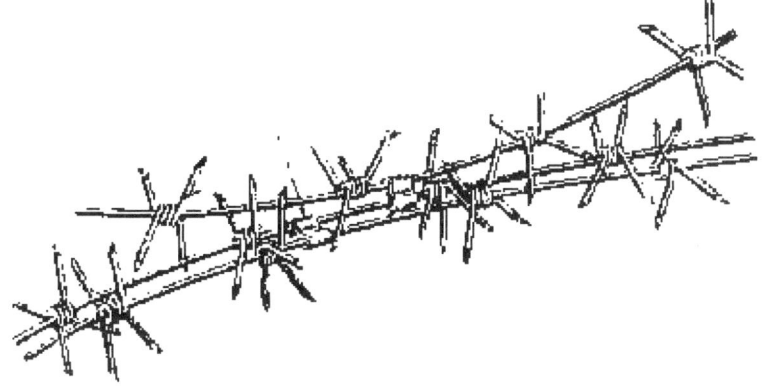

by Hermanus Knoop

INHERITANCE PUBLICATIONS
NEERLANDIA, ALBERTA, CANADA
PELLA, IOWA, U.S.A.

National Library of Canada Cataloguing in Publication Data

Knoop, Herm. (Herman), 1891-1974.
  A theatre in Dachau

  Translation of: Een theater in Dachau.
  ISBN 0-921100-20-5

  1. World War, 1939-1945—Personal narratives, Dutch. 2. Dachau
(Concentration camp) 3. World War, 1939-1945—Religious aspects. I.
Title.
  D805.5.D33K5613 2001   940.53'174336   C2001-911488-5

Library of Congress Cataloging-in-Publication Data

(Applied for — not available at time of printing)

LC Control Number: 2001006114

Translated by Andrew Petter
Edited by Roelof A. Janssen
Cover design by Roelof A. Janssen

Box 154, Neerlandia, Alberta Canada T0G 1R0
Tel. & Fax (780) 674 3949
Web site: http://www.telusplanet.net/public/inhpubl/webip/ip.htm
E-Mail inhpubl@telusplanet.net

Published simultaneously in U.S.A. by Inheritance Publications
Box 366, Pella, Iowa 50219

Available in Australia from Inheritance Publications
Box 1122, Kelmscott, W.A. 6111 Tel. & Fax (089) 390 4940

ISBN 0-921100-20-5

Printed in Canada

Table of Contents

De Gevangene

Hij vreesde niet die 't lichaam kunnen dooden,
Langzaam, langzaam moordend in een cel,
Of met de kogel, zakelijk en snel.
Hij sprak, wat Gij hem hadt geboden.

Nu hebben zij hem in hun kooi gevangen,
Maar biddend zingt zijn ziel zich los, en vrij,
Ver boven haat en spot en medelij,
Is hij ontvlucht tot U, zijn diepst verlangen.

Zij kunnen binden — 't Woord blijft ongebonden,
Zij kunnen dooden — de Verlosser leeft,
En wie Hij van Zijn Geest gegeven heeft,
Die leeft met Hem, bevrijd van band' en zonden.

Zoo doe G'ons allen deze troost ervaren,
Die sterkt in smaad en spot en eenzaamheid,
Want wie om Christus' wille smaadheid lijdt,
Dien zult Gij tot in eeuwigheid bewaren.
— Mevr. C.E.T. Luykenaar Francken-Schreuder

The Prisoner

He did not fear those who could kill the body,
Slowly murdering him in prison,
Or with a bullet, businesslike and quick;
He spoke that which Thou to him had bidden.

Now they have caught him in their cage.
But by singing prayer he frees his soul
Far above all hatred, mocking, and sympathy,
He flees to Thee, his highest goal.

They can bind — but the Word stays free;
They can kill — but the Saviour lives.
And with Him, freed of sin and ties,
Live those to whom He of His Spirit gives.

Thus grant all of us this comfort,
Which strengthens while mocked in loneliness.
For he who suffers for the sake of Christ.
Thou wilt preserve in eternal blessedness.
— Mrs. C.E.T. Luykenaar Francken-Schreuder
(Translated by Roelof A. Janssen)

Editor's Preface

The present book is a thoroughly edited and re-translated version of the text as it was published in *Concordia* (a Protestant Reformed periodical) in 1947 and 1948. Since the original translation was done by Rev. Andrew Petter, we believe he should have the honour of being referred to as translator. However, as editor, I had to translate several passages which were missing (sometimes a few paragraphs but also one or more missing installments), and also make hundreds of editorial changes. Thus I take full responsibility for the final text.

— Roelof A. Janssen

Preface by Dr. Klaas Schilder

It was a quiet evening when the author of this book and I returned our thoughts to Dachau. It was not the first time. Time and time again we remembered those many to whom we felt attached because of ecclesiastical or other ties, who had been murdered there. Murdered by the revolutionaries. Murdered by those diseasing minds, whose uniformed skeleton-delegates had picked up the *Myths* of Alfred Rosenberg from my room in August 1940, but who were actually possessed by those *Myths* themselves. Also picked up at that time were the articles on the German church conflict by H.W. Van der Vaart Smit. In reality [according to H.W. Van der Vaart Smit and other National Socialists —Editor] there had not been a church conflict in Germany at all.

It was a quiet evening, but our wandering thoughts had to go back even further than Dachau. That "wandering" found in this "necessary task" its natural end. For indeed, as often as the students of the apostolic author, who had — already twenty centuries before the atomic bomb — opened their eyes to the fact that the end of the world had come upon them, think of those brothers who completed their race in Dachau, their thoughts will only be able to stay on *their proper course* if they recall that great cloud of witnesses which has existed ever since the blood of Abel began to cry out.

So our thoughts wandered in a direct line back to Paul, the great witness of Jesus Christ. It was he who confronted the martyrs of Jesus Christ of every century with their brute persecutors. He also confronted the saturated, self-satisfied, and self-centred side of the Church, which existed even in times of persecution. And he was the one who turned the fine irony of the fourth chapter of the first letter to the Church at Corinth into a weapon of God's Spirit against the full satisfaction of the average vegetating church member. Was there such an upper-class community residing in Corinth? Perhaps, but once again Paul inspects his work clothes, which at times were exchanged for the jail clothes which the prison guard in the jail of Rome's totalitarian state regularly supplied him with. What about his identification card? He did not have it with him in prison. He was only a type of example. And as regards this type, it has always been called "the scum of the world," everyone's "garbage." He sat on the lowest seat, in the row of those who were condemned with him. And thus he, an apostle, an ambassador of the King of kings, Jesus Christ, became a spectacle for the world and for men and for angels. A spectacle! Whoever wants to see it, and has the time for it, can enjoy it.

A spectacle! In the Greek it is called, "a theatre."

Paul chose his examples carefully. The cultured Greek man was fond of the theatre; the beautiful rich harbour city of Corinth would certainly have wanted to maintain its elevated place by granting a theatre within its walls. Kittel shows us that this same word "theatre" takes its course in classical literature. A theatre can be the *building* in which the play is performed, or it can mean the *audience in the auditorium*. However, there is still a third meaning, that of 1 Cor. 4:9. Here theatre means *the play itself*, the play for which the audience has come to visit the building.

A performance of a dramatic play is to be given, but who is the director? The Director is God. And who are the audience? They are the world, men, and angels. And what is the play? It is the drama of the suffering, persecution, and destruction of Christ's faithful servants, whom the prince of this world struck, and struck hard. They suffered hunger and thirst. They were put in prison and in the concentration camp. They were caned and their backs were ripped open. Their names became infamous. They became fools, pitiable people. Their position was impossible.

And all of this was done in public. Just as the Roman magistrates and people rushed together in marching order whenever Christians were sacrificed in the arenas, so Paul and his evangelists and other colleagues became a spectacle, a *public theatre*.

Some have wondered whether the apostle, in his figurative language, was using a popular philosophical term, or as we would say, a fashionable slogan of the vocabulary of the public university of those days. It is not impossible. This author has more than once demonstrated that he was so "Spirit-wise" he seemed spirited. He knew his Grecians and their "Grecianisms," and he spoke to them in their own language, especially in their "cultural centres," as they called their cities.

Scholars arrived at this idea because of the favourite imagery of the "stoic philosophers," which was the idea that the wise man — the proud philosopher of liberty and self-sufficiency — became a spectacle, a theatre, "for gods and men" in his battle with "fate." Such a spectacle, that is, such a dramatic play, was not too low for the residents of heaven: a courageous man fighting against fate. What could be stronger, more conscious, and more beautiful than the philosopher of human self-sufficiency, the man who above all things enjoys his liberty?

It is possible that Paul had heard various phrases of these stoic philosophers, and that his quick-witted spirit had picked up their theme in his finely ironical dialogue with the Christian people in that conceited Corinth. But, even if this was the case, Paul was still the exact opposite of the heathen humanist of Greece. The principled stoic honours the beautiful, strong man who, by his own dominion over his destiny and life — and especially over himself — prepares a pure joy: In the theatre of man, the gods can come and behold . . . their equals!

But for Paul it was not the self-sufficient human who directed the performance of a play, an idea entirely of man's own imagination, and for that reason, made of such spontaneous ability in perception that it made *the divine aristocratic gift of human beings* the permanent theme. Indeed not. For Paul it was God Himself who directed the play. Only God is self-sufficient and complete in Himself. To His creation, also to man, He granted in that creation, or re-granted in the re-creation, a created self-sufficiency — a satisfaction, a contentment, a happy disposition — which was not present at birth, but was given by grace, and which did not boast of what was in man or attached to man, but in what his God had given him by grace. So that now, in complete opposition to the stoic, no flesh would boast before Him, and none of the philosophers, for example, men like Paul or one of his Corinthian students, would become conceited in his office, as if he was a self-sufficient, spontaneous person with a self-sufficiency drawn out of his own power. Therefore, if God's apostle-philosophers desire to remain in the school of Paul, He gives them "a thorn in the flesh." He allows them to be hit by fists. He throws the prison gates open for them Himself. He even lets them be butchered, so that His children will know and experience that the Book of Job is not a theatre-play from a gray past, with scenes from Uz and dramatists who carry those real old-fashioned Jewish names. No, He shows that the Book of Job continues to be experienced in that the Word of God comes to pass every day. In the theatre-play of Job, the Word of God shows that man is but a creature, and that he will have to lay his hand over his mouth when God demonstrates to him that He is *faithful to Himself.*

He demonstrates that *He* is faithful to Himself.

He is faithful to Himself as Judge and as Avenger. Yes, then man can speak of *disaster.* However, he will not do it down here.

But He is *also* faithful to Himself as *Father in the Lord Christ,* and as Perseverer in His saints, Perseverer in faithfulness to Himself, because those who are His are made to persevere in faithfulness to Him. Then man can speak of *fortune,* even in his *misfortune.* Then he can speak of great salvations, even in the greatest disasters. Then he has become a theatre, this man with his sores and wounds. Then God Himself will not come to that play in surprise. Did He not write the narrative Himself, before the foundation of the world was laid? No, He is the Director. The *world,* *men,* and *angels* may come to *see* it.

The world, men, and angels. That means all creatures. The suffering of God's embassy is a public court case, just as the dispute of the LORD against the covenant congregation of Micah 6 was a public court case. In a public court case, God wants to prove to all creatures — to angels above and evil angels below, and to all people, good and evil — that He will persevere in those who are His. He proves this so that those angels and the people who, through the death of Christ, receive by faith the peace which is universal throughout the world, will know that the righteous will be saved, even though they are molested. They receive by grace created self-sufficiency, the knowledge that they will through God persevere in God. He also proves this in order that those other angels and people, who celebrate the stoic self-sufficiency as having come from humanistically easy-going self-obtained goods — and who also invite the gods to their celebration — as yet will hear the question, "If the righteous will not even be saved without being molested, where then will the ungodly and sinner appear?"

These are not laurel-crowned heroes, but wounded slaves. These are the people in the play which God, the Father of the Crucified One, is directing in this world-theatre. "Step forward," He calls, "step forward and behold what I meant when I caused My apostle, My number-one figure in the drama, to write that he was filling up in his own body the left-over suffering of My Son. I caused him to be lifted up from the earth first, to be publicly condemned in order that thus sin might be fully rebuked for its insolent boast of owing nothing and being wholly self-sufficient."

In the deepest sense, those who beat men into insanity with the lash, reached for the deadly hypodermic needle, or sent men off to the gas-chamber at Dachau were not "Germans." They were the heroes of the world-drama. They were the drunken followers of Alfred Rosenberg. They at least had read and thoroughly learned the philosophy of pride, the philosophy of Germanic idealism, of the teachers of the typical German Freedom-philosophy. In their "culture," their "religion," and their philosophical reflections, their "god" had become "God." They had glorified (as god) their totalitarian state, which spontaneously and automatically, from within itself, contained and enclosed all Right, and brought this Right to its proper effect in its power-expansion, and did so in and through its own offspring.

And thus they thrust at God, God who is Law-Giver from above. And thus they struck at His servants. This was a theatre, to their way of thinking; and although all the people were not exactly permitted to look behind the scene, yet their German "god," who had come to embodiment and consciousness in themselves, was learning the theatrical art through them. This totalitarian "god" was actually scourging through their hand. He was actually pushing the pen that listed the death candidates for each day. And as they stood there in the torture-chamber, gloating and snickering, their sadistic grip was really that of their German "god" who had come to look on with them at the drama which they were staging. He laughed along with them. Pantheists and mysticists cannot, of course, see anything strange in the fact that directing a play and going to see a play are really one and the same thing. All freedom philosophers, stoic-born, Hegelian-oriented people must come to the oneness of the world and the Satanist, and also the oneness of the drama and the dramatist.

But anyone who has become really small because he has grown up by the word of the Apostle Paul, is deeply conscious of the fact that there is a real difference between the drama of time and the great Dramatist who has formed and chosen him. He knows that it is God who is directing the play in Rome, in Ephesus, in Doornik (where Guido de Brès died —Editor), in Dachau, and everywhere else. Hence, he is not disturbed when he sees the hangman, helper of Satan and the Beast, come forward. The play is following the plan, according to the Divine prescription. And His eternal good pleasure prescribed this. What harm can then befall them?

> *Although my flesh and heart may fail,*
> *God is my strength, I shall prevail,*
> *For He, whose steadfast love is sure,*
> *Will be my portion evermore.*

And what if the world stands near to observe the show? What if their carcasses are hauled to the cremation room? Or what if they retain breath in their lungs just long enough to still be caught in all their nakedness on some film about Dachau? Come what may, let it be seen in the play. Those who are for them, are more than those who are against them.[1] There is also a prayer-service being held on their behalf in heaven, according to the fifth seal. That heavenly prayer-service is really a drama, a drama from beginning to end. That service does not merely show what lives in the hearts of those heavenly beings. No, that service is action. It strives towards a definite goal. That service brings about the coming of Jesus Christ. It works as instrument and as condition of that coming. And so we have in Dachau a theatre!

It is a minister of the Word whose thoughts we have before us in this book. He is one among those who have proved themselves faithful to the decisions of a synod. To the decision of the Synod of the Reformed (*Gereformeerd*) Churches of 1936, regarding those members who were adherents to the principles of the *Nationaal Socialistische Beweging* (Dutch Nazi Party). And to that other decision, namely, that the Christian should pray for the head of

---

[1] The allusion is to the host of angels that Elisha saw in the mountain tops in a time of danger. See 2 Kings 6:16-17. —Trans.

14

his state, Queen Wilhelmina of Orange, who remained head of the state even during the German occupation. A decision that men should pray that prayer publicly, in the arena, in the theatre for the world and for angels and for men.

There are also those who sabotaged these decisions of the Synod. They were found among the very people who had made proclamation of these decisions, and who, when certain other decisions[2] came into dispute, stubbornly "maintained" these latter decisions, even though it meant suspension and deposition from office, which office was regarded altogether too much from the view-point of human privilege. Their suspending of these persons they held forth as an important phase in the theatre before angels and men. But they did not even step forward to the defence of the author of the present book.

But God was leading the attack among those who helped in this distress. And among those who here offered help were numbered — among many others — those other Gospel-ministers who were made a display and were murdered in Dachau, ministers who had also remained faithful to these decisions which were sabotaged by the others. The author also makes mention of them. They are the pastors Kapteyn, Sietsma, and Tunderman. These God took away. Thus it was required in the role that was written for them in God's theatre at Dachau. And now their brother in the faith, whose time was not yet fulfilled, comes to us to pass on to us something of the good Word of God which strengthened, built, and perfected them in their fellowship with each other, daily disrupted though it often was.

Let us, then, read with tense interest of spirit. For I consider that God has set us, the Apostles, forth, last of all, as men doomed to die. The time will not be long before a new woe overtakes us. For we continue to be a theatre in the world. "But recall the former days, in which, after you . . . were made a spectacle (theatre) both by reproaches and tribulation" (Hebrews. 10:32, 33), in order that the new theatre-play may not take you unawares as a thief in the night, in order that your lamps may be found burning, inasmuch as the Bridegroom comes. Behold He comes quickly. And with Him is His reward.

— K. Schilder

---

[2] The well-known decision of the Synods 1939-1943 (Sneek & Utrecht) and 1943-1945 (Utrecht), which were the cause for the Liberation of 1944. —Trans.

1. A Door Closed Behind Me

On Wednesday, November 19, 1941, at about 1:30 P.M., the door of cell 25 of the police station at the Haagsche Veer in Rotterdam locked behind me. The Gestapo had finally closed in and I was in the clutches of the Beast. *A prisoner for the Word of God and for the Testimony of Jesus Christ.* It was by orders of the head of the German Security Police that I was arrested. This being taken into custody had been preceded by a final interrogation, very unpleasant at times, lasting about three hours. Neither party would give quarter. The Gestapo officer who was questioning me declined to yield and I also on my part refused to yield. It was definitely a question of who should win this contest, he or I. And I lost, at least in appearance; and he won, that is also in appearance. He won as regards the external conflict, because he had the power; I lost even though I had the right on my side.

Now, although the possibility of being released from custody presented itself during this last interrogation, I did not consider myself justified to take advantage of it. For I did not regard it justifiable before God to return to freedom as a "bound" man and thus be under the necessity of living a life of freedom as a bound man. By doing that I would have bartered away the liberty with which Christ had made me free. But I also declined the opportunity of seizing this chance of freedom because I realized very well that if I should ever again be summoned, I would in advance have forfeited and lost every right of testifying to my faith. How would I, who had sold my liberty in Christ "for a morsel of meat" in order to buy a "liberty" without Christ, later be able to defend my spiritual freedom in Christ with confidence and without shame. I was determined to preserve that freedom and not to sell it to a power which was waging war against Christ, and which, according to the description of Psalm 2, was engaged in the great battle of the ages which takes council against the LORD and against His Christ saying, "Let us break their bonds in pieces and cast their cords from us."

And, moreover, who would give me a guarantee that the present offer of liberty was not simply a trap to evoke a decision from me which would be dishonouring to the Name of the Lord, and which would not avail me because it was already definitely decided, no matter what happened, to withdraw me from circulation? The only way that I could pursue was the way of faith; I can do nothing else, so help me God! And that is the way I have taken.

The seizure of that unforgettable day did not, however, come unexpectedly. Long before this I was not only prepared for the worst, but I was prepared and ready. I saw the moment coming ever nearer after each encounter with the German Security Police. I had consequently taken the necessary preparatory measures on the evening before the 19th of November. Considering the possibility that my arrest would take place on the 19th, and that most probably my home would be subject to a search, I destroyed the "illegal" papers which were in my possession, among which was also a second article prepared for an "illegal" magazine of which I had become a contributor. By letter I took leave of my consistory and congregation.[3] By means of prayer, my wife and I prepared ourselves for what we were sure was awaiting us on the morrow.

---

[3] The following is the Letter of Farewell to the congregation:

Rotterdam, Nov. 18, 1941

Esteemed Gentlemen and Brothers,

Since now has happened that which I had already long expected, and for which I had kept myself in complete readiness, namely, that I have been placed under arrest by the German authorities, I need to write you.

It is my firm conviction that this has befallen me for the sake of the Name and the cause of the Lord. And I deem it an honour that Christ the Lord has counted me worthy of being bound for this cause. You must not think that this is easy for me. It is hard for me to relinquish this work which is very dear to me; especially hard since it is in these times so necessary for the congregation to have the Scriptures opened to her with a view to the threatening spiritual dangers, and it was a joy to me to be busy lighting her way by the Scriptures through these times, so that she might be steadfast, immovable, always abounding in the work of the Lord, knowing that her labour is not in vain in the Lord. Apparently the Lord has willed this way with me. May He do as seems good in His eyes.

I have always marvelled at the fact that my arrest did not take place long before. It remains a riddle to me that the authorities suffered me to stand so long, in contrast with some of my colleagues who were sometimes arrested after preaching only one sermon. In the various interrogations I had certainly not soft-pedalled my convictions. For I had already been involved with the German Security Police for a full year, ever since November 1940. I had been questioned by them at least six times during that year.

And besides these six interrogations by the Germans, I had also been questioned twice by the so-called Dutch Police, by its political branch at the main building in the Haagsche Veer. As much as I resented appearing repeatedly before those Germans for interrogation, still greater was my repulsion against being compelled to appear before those cowardly underlings who brought the Dutch police into such discredit, namely, the N.S.B.[4] traitors. The Germans were at least the enemies of my land and people, but these "Dutchmen" — who held themselves forth as patriots

---

It is also a great grief to me that because of my arrest I am hindered from instructing my catechumens in the "aforesaid doctrine," to visit the sick, and to participate in the work of the consistory. May the Lord give me grace to relinquish all these things as long as it pleases Him. May He grant that we soon may see one another again. And may He be very near unto us also in the hour of temptation, that we may be strong in and through Him. And should we never see one another again, then I must thank you sincerely for all the love, interest, help, and support that I have experienced from you in your midst.

I have enjoyed the good among you.

I would still make this one request of you: Kindly do not forget my wife in her loneliness. Support her with your prayers, and the expression of your interest and concern for her. I commit her to your brotherly love. She has no one besides myself.

And remember me also in your prayers, both in your meetings and worship, and in your family prayers.

May the Lord speedily bring us together again, and may He be gracious to His Church, our people, and country, and to our royal family.

Cordially, with fraternal greetings, your devoted Brother in Christ,

— Hermanus Knoop

[4] N.S.B. is the convenient abbreviation for *Nationaal Socialistische Beweging* (National Socialistic Movement). Dutch Nazism became a very strong movement in The Netherlands before the war. It would prove to be a kind of fifth column as soon as the war broke out. See Klaas Schilder, *Geen Duimbreed* (Kampen: Kok, 1936).

— Trans.

par excellence, whereas they had in fact done nothing less than betray their native land and deliver many of their own countrymen into the hand of the enemy — these people I could only despise. As we shall also see later, they would soon play me into the hands of the Germans.

But now, on November 19, 1941, it was the last day of those often very grueling interrogations. The Gestapo closed in. I was in the clutch of the Beast *for the Word of God and for the Testimony of Jesus Christ*. And this was to no other purpose than that I should become a theatre to the world and to angels and to men. And so it was that the door of cell number 25 locked behind me.

2. Preliminaries to My Arrest: Immediate Resistance for Christ's Sake

In our home on the evening of the sad day of May 14, 1940, when our army had no choice but to capitulate (thanks to the overwhelming power of the hordes of the German barbarians, and to the dastardly bombardment of Rotterdam, and also thanks to the foul treachery of certain unpatriotic Dutch scoundrels), my wife and I spoke in deep dejection of the affliction that was about to overtake our land and people, and of the future of our people; in the midst of that conversation I stated, "That means the concentration camp for me sooner or later."

What was it that caused me to assert this with such a great feeling of certainty? Was it an expression of spiritual pedantry, or self-conceit, or of an over-estimation of self? I do not believe so. Let me try to make plain whereon that firm conviction on my part was based.

When Germany began her war against Poland, and also France and England became involved, I had no doubt but that The Netherlands would also become involved with Germany. The Nazi beast had broken loose and was out for booty. For the Nazi monster there would be no boundaries where it would cease to satisfy its greedy hunger. Also The Netherlands, despite its assurances, or rather just because of its assurances, would not be spared. And it was fully evident that no matter how courageous and stubborn a defence we presented, we would be unable to hold out against such a colossus. That meant a National Socialistic invasion into our country with all its results. But that also meant that it would be the imperative duty of faith to sound the call to spiritual resistance.

Therefore, when the capitulation of our army also became a fact on that gloomy May 14 of 1940, I was convinced that the principle occupation of our land would not be that of soldiers from the Third Reich, but would be an occupation by its National Socialistic ideology, life, and worldview. For the military occupation would irrevocably bring with it the importation of a National Socialistic regime into our country and the dominion of all its principles over our people in all the spheres of their existence. Germany would take a monopoly for its ideology on every last little area of the spiritual, moral, and social life of our country and people.

The insatiable Nazi beast would engulf and swallow up everything, and all who might try to resist that process would be trampled to pieces by its feet. Now I believed that this would bring with it the greatest dangers for our church and state and society, and the most fatal consequences. Was not Germany itself our most telling example and warning in this respect? Where this National Socialism established its power, that is its tyranny, there was nothing left for the Church and Christendom but a total and radical retreat, until it was brought into an impasse where no choice remained except unconditional surrender or a battle to the death. And this choice meant for our people, as to their Christian element, that those things which they had, in faithfulness and obedience to the principles gathered from the Scriptures, built up through years of struggle, would now have to fall under the sledge-hammer blows of this outright pagan regime which is an enemy of death to the Church and Christendom. Indeed, this Nazi regime could not tolerate even the slightest form of Christian life in our society, but would necessarily have to eradicate it. And thus it could not be but that this domination which had imposed itself on our free people in that fatal hour, would necessarily lead to the total paganization of the life of our people. This National Socialism would not tolerate principles which stood diametrically opposed to it, but would destroy them to the last remnant. It would not be stopped at any boundary-line in its crusade of principles.

It moved forward according to its plan — and the end of its campaign of conquest was the exercise of complete and sole domination over the spirits of all who were brought under its yoke. Whoever would not think and act according to the spirit of National Socialism was an arch-enemy, and his lot was annihilation.

With all these things clearly before my eyes, the question forced itself upon me: What now was my duty in these changed circumstances, both as a citizen of this Dutch nation, and as one called by the grace of God to give spiritual leadership? What was my calling now?

Already years before May 10, 1940, I had seen it as my calling to warn the Reformed Christians, among whom the Lord had been pleased to appoint me my life's task, against the spiritual dangers which threatened from the direction of National Socialism, which was also in our land beginning to beat its drum and was engaged in infecting our people with its *authoritarian* principles. And I felt this calling so much the more because I discovered those in my own circle, and that not the least in the upper class, who were actually charmed by this ideology, and who began to labour zealously with practical means for it. I warned with cutting sharpness; according to some, to the point of nausea, and according to others, to extremes, because it was not as bad as I represented it and it would most probably fizzle out. But by the grace of God and in the consciousness of my duty to fulfil my prophetic calling, looking away from the judgments of men, I have continued to warn and to summon to faithfulness to proper principles, according to the Word.

It stands to reason, then, that on that May 14, 1940, the question of my duty pressed itself upon me. Ah, there were so many possibilities! There was the possibility to yield and to capitulate to this spiritual enemy and to let rest the struggle and the warnings against this anti-Christian life and worldview under the present circumstances. That would mean *desiring to save one's life*. Would that be permissible for me? Even though there was plenty of truth to preach besides these things? Would it be permissible, driven by the foolish urge of self-preservation — which of course is only an illusion — to permit bounds to be set to our prophetic witness? There was also another possibility, namely, to at least begin to offer some resistance, but if things should begin to become tense, and danger begin to threaten, then to retire step by step, to execute some spiritual withdrawal-moves, to shorten the front. Would such a thing be justified before God and His Church? And would I, then, be faithfully fulfilling my calling? Would I thus be keeping the vow that I had made at the time I accepted the office of a preacher of the Word? The end would then, nevertheless, mean unconditional surrender. Was I allowed to do that? Were not the most precious things of life at stake? Was it in such a situation justified *to save one's life*, thus to permit our prophetic testimony to sound forth ever weaker, until at last it ended in silence?

There was one other possibility that presented itself. This, namely, to simply draw the line through consistently as in the days before. That would mean both to undertake resistance for the faith myself, and to arouse others to resistance. Fully aware of the implications, that evening I took the decision to begin this resistance regardless of the consequences for me. For not my little cause or our little cause was in dispute here, but that great and most weighty cause in all the world, the cause of the Church of the Lord, and the Kingdom of God, of the Gospel of Jesus Christ. For that cause I had to remain faithful, had to stand in my prophetic calling and unmovably so. I had to obey God rather than any man. Here there was only room for the child-like obedience of faith that knows: "He who will lose his life for My sake and, for the sake of the Gospel, shall save it."

I repeat that I was, from the beginning, deeply conscious that this would bring with itself the most serious consequences for me. And not only that. But I was also, from the beginning, ready to bear the consequences. Ah, for one who lives out of faith, things are so different. For is not the content of his faith *God*? Through that faith we are equal to all things: just because through God we are equal to all things, and He is the content of our faith. And by faith we can do all things we are *called* to do; there are no hindrances. For just as the power of God, who is the content of our faith, is unlimited, so also the power of the possession of faith is unlimited. That faith dares to do all that it is called to do. If it stands before a wall, high and insurmountable, it does not stand there, but with God he who has faith and uses his faith, leaps over it. Then he who truly lives out of faith is always prepared to bear the extreme consequences. Because I lived by faith, therefore I was prepared and equal to bear the most serious consequences of my spiritual resistance. For it would concern the word of God and the testimony of Jesus, and these are worthy of the greatest sacrifice.

But there was something more. It appeared to me far from imaginary that the highly renowned National Socialistic coordination method would be carried out just as subtly in our country as it had been done in Germany itself. And that thus, if we did not keep our eyes wide open, the process would be completed before we were really aware of it. It was, therefore, essential, not only that we ourselves should be continually in readiness to begin immediate spiritual resistance, but also to urge others to readiness for resistance. Therefore I had decided to call others to this resistance for the faith and to this spiritual struggle, lest by any means even the smallest symptom of this National Socialistic influence should take control of the life of the Church, and thus also of the life of the people. Thus I desired to keep the Church pure if possible. And that not only for the sake of the Church, but also for the sake of my people. For the situation is thus, that *he who keeps the Church pure, thereby serves his countrymen*; *for he keeps his people pure*. Betrayal of the Church always means, at the same time, betrayal of one's country, and vice-versa. Who among our people would presently prove to be the betrayers of their country? Who but the betrayers of the Church? And who would reveal themselves as the betrayers of the Church? Who other than the traitors to their country?[5]

Thus I hoped, that by beginning resistance for the faith within the churches, in which I was privileged to serve, I might also move others to that resistance. For the believer is admonished, instructed, and strengthened in his three-fold office exactly in the assembly of the congregation of Christ. Thus strengthened he may go out from the assembly of the believing Church and enter into the various relationships of life. Thus he will be activated in his offices by the testimony of the Holy Spirit, in order that he may be active as prophet, confessing the name of God in word and

---

[5] This became very evident in the Reformed (*Gereformeerd*) weekly *De Heraut* (The Herald), which, under the editor-in-chief, Dr. H.H. Kuyper, provided leadership in a manner that betrayed Church and State.

deed; as priest, who offers himself as an oblation of gratitude and to intercede for others; and as king, who carries the battle against all powers that oppose themselves against the LORD and against His Anointed. To be of service in this activation to spiritual resistance was my heartfelt desire.

I also took into account the fact that it was very well possible that cooperation from others would be lacking even in my own circle, possibly from considerations of cowardice, or from the wisdom of serpents, but in any event, from lack of sufficient faith, absence of faith, or from the failure to make use of faith. In fact, at that time I took into vivid account the fact that I might possibly have to fight against those who held themselves forth as "*leaders*" of our Reformed people, but who, nevertheless, did not derive this claim from their Scriptural consciousness of their calling, but from the fact that they had grasped the opportunity of elbowing their way to the top, and had gained a leader's seat. I was aware that I might even have to warn the Reformed people against those whom they considered their leaders, and had until now honoured as leaders, and followed faithfully, since these would actually prove to lead them astray. Thus I foresaw the possibility of a conflict: On the one hand, with the power of occupation through its Gestapo, and on the other hand, a conflict with my own fellow-believers. Thus a battle-front towards the outside, and also one directed towards the inside would be drawn.

How clear and vivid these reflections of May 14, 1940, still stand in my mind after these five years. And it was with all this in mind that I could say to my wife on that eventful evening, "That means the concentration camp for me sooner or later."

How I have wrestled with the Lord in prayer that I might remain faithful to the task of my prophetic office in this situation!

3. The Call to Resistance for the Faith for the Word of God

Since it was now a settled question in my mind that my spiritual resistance must begin immediately, the next question was in what way and by what means this must be accomplished. I considered it to be wholly justifiable and my imperative duty to stay awake, and to further arouse that portion of the Reformed people within my reach, and to urge them on to the resistance for the faith by means of the preaching and the press.

As concerned the press, I had at my disposal my congregation's church bulletin, known as the *Delfshavensche Kerkbode*. This bulletin appeared, naturally, only once a week, and was, of course, not very large. And since the Reformed (*Gereformeerd*) congregation of Rotterdam-Delfshaven was served by four pastors, who each took the editorship for a month in turn, I would have the use of this means of expression only one month in four. That was not much, of course. Still I considered it my duty to make use of this limited means in order that within the sphere of my official calling and competency, I might give the leadership which I considered necessary. And I hoped that what I considered myself called by God to speak of, might also be heard outside of my limited sphere of labour. I therefore made use of this means with the consequence — as we shall see later — that this bulletin was prohibited twice.

As regards the other means, namely, my preaching, every Sunday I had the pulpit at my disposal with opportunity to proclaim to the congregation what I considered necessary, by virtue of my official mandate from Christ. Therefore I made ready use of this opportunity. However, I was convinced that what I might and must proclaim from the pulpit must remain within the bounds of the Gospel message. For, let us not forgot that the pulpit is not the place for a political agitator; the assembly of the saints is no political gathering, and the minister of the Word is no political debater. Hence, my calling was not to conduct "political action" from my pulpit in the midst of the assembled congregation. That would surely be a violation. My calling was limited within the bounds of the competency which the Lord Jesus Christ had given to the offices, namely, to let the light of the Word of God shine on public life in all its relationships and on whatever activities that life brought to view. The Church preaches *principles*, very concretely and very timely. Within the limits of this official competence I therefore tried to administer my prophetic office and to apply the keys of the Kingdom of Heaven in accordance with the duty of my office, as the Church confesses it in the Heidelberg Catechism, Lord's Day 31.

Again, I did this to arouse the congregation and keep her awake, that she might see by what danger she, and with her, all of Christendom, was threatened in the National Socialistic ideology which was about to become dominant. She was to be aroused so that not a single Christian should dance to its tune or should mourn to its lamentation, but that wisdom, the wisdom of the antithesis, which may never become unfashionable or crumble away, might be justified in her children. I hoped that an unmoveable and strong stability and a willingness to carry out the sacrifice of life itself, for the sake of Christ and His Gospel, might become manifest.

In the various interrogations to which the Gestapo officer subjected me, I tried to make plain my perception and position concerning the calling and task of the Minister of the Word. Again and again he would bring up the simplistic accusation that I had "brought politics" into the pulpit. And everything which did not concern itself with the "soul" belonged, according to his thinking, to "politics." The Church and its preaching must concern itself only with that which pertains to the "soul" of man. All that lay outside of this did not concern her. That belonged to the sphere of the state.

Although I tried, with emphasis, to make him see that, according to our Reformed understanding, the ministry of the Word in the assembly of the congregation of Christ could only exist by its own proper principle, and that with this principle it stands or falls, my repeated efforts were all in vain. It did not make a difference to him how the Church, and especially those Reformed people, thought about it. As for me, I was simply to hold myself to the principle of German National Socialism, namely, that religion is a matter of the Church since it is a matter of the soul; and that Church, religion, Bible, and the message of proclamation, had nothing to do with all that which lies outside of the religion-for-the-soul. And thus our conversation on this issue ran aground every time again.

This same unbiblical and hence rejected concept was also proclaimed to me by the official of the "political branch" of the so-called Dutch Police. This disciple literally repeated the words of his pay-master. He went even further than his master by saying that the Church's only task was to train customers for heaven, and beyond this she had no business in any other sphere. Thus it was perfectly fair that anyone who, in spite of repeated warnings, set his ecclesiastical feet on territory reserved for the state and its functionaries, should merit a terrible punishment. Such a one would also certainly receive it. So for him the discussion always ran stuck on the question of the *own proper principle* of the preaching of the Word.

Moreover, it soon became evident that there was a lamentable need to convince my own congregation of this calling and competency of the preaching of the Gospel in accord with its own given principles. To this end I made use of the church bulletin, the *Delfshavensche Kerkbode*. In the issue of October 5, 1940, I wrote a meditation on Ezekiel 33:1-7, under the title, "The Responsibility of the Watchman."[6] The necessity for me to elaborate on what I said in my preaching was becoming evident. To my astonishment I noticed that this was not superfluous. It became plain to me through all manner of conversations I had; by what was whispered around; by secret actions taken behind my back; by colleagues; by the stirring of "fellow-believers" underground. These "fellow believers" were those who were either seized in the clutches of fear, and thus did not live out of faith, but boasted of the "wisdom of serpents" as the highest wisdom; or who out of "tactful" consideration strove, no matter what the cost, to avoid a conflict with the National Socialistic occupation authority which was encroaching more and more on all of life. These all desired to save their life and its

---

[6] This Meditation emphasizes the tremendous responsibility of the Minister of the Word to discern the first inkling of threatening danger when the Lord sends the sword of trial and temptation and deception against His Church. The congregation has the right to expect of him as watchman that he shall warn them long before they themselves sense the danger. —Trans.

content for themselves; *rest* was what they desired. They wanted to see what they considered as their work, which they had produced and built, remain intact. They did not desire the cross for the sake of Christ and His Gospel. They saw that this cross and this suffering would inevitably approach if resistance for the faith was undertaken. They desired to obey man rather than God. They followed Satan rather than Christ. Thus they purposely misunderstood my purpose to carry on the principle battle of faith. They thoroughly knew this battle theoretically, but in practice they did not desire to engage in it, because they did not desire to make the sacrifice which obedience in the office of prophet, priest, and king would require. Therefore, they wished to destroy what I desired to undertake by calling it bravura, irresponsibility, or recklessness. To secure his own safety beforehand, one colleague declared that if I became imprisoned he would not be able to pray for me. And thus to my dismay I was confronted with the fact that all manner of beautiful principles were confessed, but that these had not become flesh and blood in many who confessed and advocated them. There was a great gulf between theory and practice, doctrine and life, in the case of spiritual shepherds, not to speak of others. They loved life and the things of life more than Christ. In the case of many of the spiritual leaders, there was little trace of that simple and childlike obedience which keeps its eye fixed on the command-ment and thus acts.

Political calculation and diplomatic manoeuvres *abounded*; the Church of God was brought into confusion. Therefore I wrote the meditation mentioned above. I desired to have the congregation see that what I was doing was *nothing unusual*; it was nothing other than the simple and childlike obedience to our prophetic calling as God required it of us who were watchmen appointed by Christ over His Church. Nothing more! However, I felt that it was not enough to emphasize this task and responsibility of the watchman.

There was another evil that began to show itself very strongly. Far from imaginary was the danger that this evil could easily penetrate all too deeply into the situation. I mean the evil of *keeping silent*. As a special attitude of wisdom, the policy of silence was being lauded. Now it so happened that my attention had fallen on the ironical word of the prophet Amos. Chapter 5:13 reads: "Therefore the prudent shall keep silent in that time, for it is an evil time." In a meditation on this passage I felt called to answer the "prudent" who appeared on the scene. This I placed in the October 26, 1940 church bulletin, under the title, "Silence?"[7]

---

[7] Silence?

Amos was an annoying character. Prophets always are. They are specialists in disturbing the sweet and blessed reposeful life of the people. Hence they are not popular, but rather the contrary. You will have to avoid them somewhat if you wish to continue your course. They always have some censure to express. You have just nicely established contact with your own flesh and the world, when, behold, sure enough, one of these fault-finding prophets must spoil the party.

That is how Israel had to get along with the prophets of the LORD, as well as with Amos. Take, for example, the word of Amos. Make no mistake: He spoke this, as is evident from his book of prophecies, in a time when *might* dominated *right*. Yes, might — His Majesty King Jeroboam himself, down to the meanest official, robbed the people. Read it, if you will, in his prophecies. And not only that, the hopelessness of the situation was that the people were simply powerless to do anything about it. The right — so decadent was life in Israel that right was nowhere to be obtained. Nowhere. They simply had to stand by helplessly and let things go their own way. How could they protest against such tyrants? It would simply mean committing suicide.

And now it seems that Amos gave some good advice. He said, "Therefore the prudent will keep silent in that time, for it is an evil time."

But you are mistaken as to the purpose of his word. For it was not *advice* that Amos gave. He merely said what he saw when he took a look around in that evil time. He saw that those who were formerly big *talkers* became silent, silent in that time of *might* triumphing over right, when arbitrary self-will swayed the sceptre. He noted this as their tactics. He called them the "prudent." Between quotation marks, you understand. We also often call such a one "prudent," and know exactly what we mean by it. They are people of *good manners*, people who know how to get along in life.

They are the talkers who have turned to silence. But why are they silent in that evil time? Is it because they comply while they still retain their own opinion? Or because they are so wonderfully pleased with the course of events? You know better. The opposite is true. It is because it is too dangerous to express their convictions. It is not advisable to speak of works with firm principle now. Self-concern holds first place in all things. They are prudent, calculating people. Indeed, there are so many of them in this world, "prudent" men of silence, who are not able to force one principled word between their lips. Let us never forget this. And let us never forget that the prophet, in mentioning this fact, intends to mark it as a *danger*, as a *sin*. He who keeps silent in the evil time out of self-concern makes the time still more evil, because might becomes still more brazen, and annihilates the last vestige of right. He who is silent out of self-concern *consents* to the evil being done. He who is silent out of self-concern approves the corruption of life. He who is silent and looks on makes himself guilty of terrible sin. He who is silent casts up no dam against evil.

Now it was both my preaching and writing, that is, my resistance for the faith for the testimony of Jesus and my arousing of others to resistance for the faith, which became the cause for which I had to appear from time to time during the full year, November, 1940 - November, 1941, before the German Security Police, and before the no less notorious "political branch" of the Rotterdam Police. The interrogations concerning that which I had written were due to the fact that the material had to be submitted for censure to some German office. The interrogations on my sermons must undoubtedly be traced to betrayal. Betrayal also from within my own Reformed circle.

4. My Defence Regarding the Accusation of Having Urged to Resist

As stated earlier, for a full year I was repeatedly called to account by the German Security Police, both for what I had written in our church bulletin and for what I had said in sermon and prayer.

I shall now tell a few things about those various interrogations, and about my defence against the accusation of having urged to resist. In these interrogations, more was said than what I am telling here, but these all concern secondary things which were not causes for my imprisonment. I am now concerned with relating the discussions which I had with the gentlemen about points of principle importance, which discussions often became very heated, and once even came near to blows.

From this account of the interrogation, it will become abundantly clear that I was, indeed, arrested *for the Word of God and for the Testimony of Jesus Christ.*

Therefore, let no one be thus prudent. Let no one be obedient to his flesh, no matter how weak, but let him stand for the truth in the evil time, and let him testify with the Word of Truth. Oh, indeed, that is "imprudent," indiscreet, But it is crucifying your "prudence" for Christ's sake. Then you may very well run into difficulties. Just look at Amos. But the most important thing must also be regarded as most important. That is God's calling, and this calling is accompanied by God's *promise*, for calling and promise are one. And the promise is that He gives liberally and does not accuse. What a blessing in an evil time for the glory of God's name you will then be.

Let me begin with the interrogations to which I had to submit because of what I had dared to write in our bulletin. My first interrogation took place in November 1940, at the office of the German Security Police, then still located at the Westplein in Rotterdam. However, before I tell about this interrogation I must call your attention to something else. It is readily understandable that after the capitulation of our army, the removal of our government to London, and the occupation of our country by the German barbarians, our people and many of the leaders were dazed. What was this that had suddenly come upon our restful, easy little life in our little Holland? In what kind of a thunderstorm had we suddenly found ourselves adrift? It was not long before we understood that we were in the hands of an enemy from whom we need expect nothing but cruelty, because he did not fear God, and thus regarded no man. No wonder that as deeply dazed as we were, we were for the moment uncertain as to which course we must pursue.

It was not long, however, before we gained our equilibrium. The Dutch level-headedness and especially the Dutch humour made their appearance again. But the Dutch business mind also awoke again very soon — the mind-set which pays attention to the business of making money without asking how. It soon became apparent how little various broad layers of our people cared about spiritual goods and what a thoroughly materialistic constitution they had. Doing business, earning money, keeping what one had and adding to it, even though the manner was not at all above suspicion — that seemed to be the highest plane to which many people could bring themselves. Thus the first daze of defeat soon made way for "caution" (wisdom). Now one may, of course, not speak disapprovingly of caution; for caution can, when it springs forth from a pure principle, spread out a rich blessing. And in such a case it may not be left unused.

However, when it does not spring from a pure principle, it must be condemned. It is an evil. And an evil tree never yields good fruit. In reality it does not merit the name which it bears. In reality it is something different. It really is shrewdness, wiliness, and diplomacy. And now this so-called caution also made its appearance in the Church of Christ, and it misled many to assume an attitude of life and deeds that became a disgrace to the Christian faith. Grievous sins were committed in the name of what was suddenly called "the wisdom of serpents." Suddenly this so-called "wisdom of serpents" became very popular, although the uprightness of doves which is mentioned by the Saviour in the same breath, was not nearly as popular. Thus one would see men yielding in the name of caution, yielding step by step and bit by bit to the pressure of the anti-Christian power of occupation. And that even with respect to the highest of possessions and values. One might see in the Christian sphere of life the most unrefreshing spectacle of men computing and calculating whether he could surrender this, or whether he could surrender that, and at the same time not cast his principles overboard, so they thought, or at least, pretended to think.

There was no common urge to resist in faith, which was able to say along the whole line, "We will *never* surrender *anything*! You are duty-bound to keep your hands off everything. We will surrender only when we are compelled by force, only after we have put up due resistance. For we must obey God rather than men."

On the other hand, there was a lamentable lack of prophetic insight and discernment. It was astounding but also very offensive to see how people simply swallowed all kinds of ordinances, complied with all kinds of demands, and failed to see them in their anti-Christian character. In this way the process of gradual coordination of our life with Nazism could not only get a start, but could also be carried through. The policy of "caution" ruled.

It soon became all too apparent that this "caution" was in fact only another word for lack of true courage in faith. This became very clearly apparent in the Christian press. Most terrible was the betrayal of principles in some of the Christian periodicals. *De Standaard* [8] (The Standard) completely changed its course in process

---

[8] *De Standaard* is famous because of Dr. Abraham Kuyper's connection with it. It was established as a Christian Daily in 1872. Dr. Kuyper was editor-in-chief for approximately forty years. In this periodical Dr. Kuyper developed his political ideas, known as Anti-Revolutionary Principles. After his retirement and even after his death (1920), it continued the tradition of Kuyper under the editorship of Prime Minister H. Colijn. Fairness and charity would seem to require of us, who do not know the details, that we do not ascribe this traitorous conduct to ex-Minister Colijn, whose perception of leadership and policy during the occupation may not always have been the wisest, but who died in German imprisonment. —Trans.

of time and permitted that traitor to his country, Max Blokzijl, to take the seat of Abraham Kuyper and Hendrik Colijn.

De Heraut (The Herald) revealed itself as a German periodical and its editor-in-chief lauded the German usurper and his administrative measures.[9]

However, the weekly periodical, *De Reformatie* (The Reformation), was from the very beginning a very favourable exception. Its editor-in-chief, Dr. Klaas Schilder, the professor at Kampen, had from the very beginning called our people, and more especially the people of our Church, to a position which was faithful to the fatherland, and which was also Scriptural. He aroused them to a strong resistance for the faith against every National Socialistic attack *on* our Christian institutions and our spiritual possessions. In a very prophetic article bearing the striking title, "Out of the Shelter, Into the Uniform," he called all people to the struggle of faith. Week after week the periodical was eagerly obtained by thousands who hungered for principled guidance and firm leadership, while they had to note, to their sorrow, how one periodical after another hauled down its banner of principle, thinking that the best way to save their existence was to help inject the poison of National Socialism into our people. Therefore the people eagerly read *De Reformatie*, rejoicing that one periodical at least dared to speak out courageously, to boldly point out what it was all about, and to stand for the cause of the living God in our land. In great suspense, people awaited every Saturday to see whether *De Reformatie* was still not prohibited.[10]

The result of this courage is well known. With the cooperation of some from among his own circle, some "Dutchmen" who collaborated with the enemy, *De Reformatie* was prohibited by the occupation-authorities, and on August 5, 1940, Dr. Schilder

---

[9] *De Heraut* is also noted because of Dr. Abraham Kuyper's long editorship. The many books which have come to us from his hand first appeared in series in *De Heraut*. To continue this tradition, his son, Prof. Dr. H.H. Kuyper, was made editor-in-chief. The author here reflects on the shameful decay of that famous Calvinistic, Reformed periodical. —Trans.

[10] For more information on the courageous stand of Dr. Klaas Schilder, see, Rudolf Van Reest, *Schilder's Struggle for the Unity of the Church*, (Neerlandia, Inheritance Publications, 1990) 231-339. —Editor.

was locked up in the House of Detention at Arnhem. By this act one of the few mouths which had still dared to speak was thus silenced.[11]

Some time after Professor Schilder was imprisoned for his faithfulness to the Church and his fatherland, another professor, namely, Dr. Van Schelven, professor at the Free University of Amsterdam, publicly revealed that he had joined the pro-German "National Front," the leader of which was Arnold Meyer. The glaring contrast between these two Reformed professors was truly quite an image of the glaring contrast which showed itself within the Reformed circle, the contrast between complete faithfulness and utter faithlessness. Now this imprisonment of one professor for his faith and the faithlessness and betrayal of the other was the occasion for my writing some articles in our church bulletin. The first article of October 5, 1940, was entitled, "Two Professors of the Little People."[12]

In the same issue of the church bulletin, I wrote an other article entitled, "No Church Conflict."[13]

---

[11] On December 16, 1940, Dr. Schilder was suddenly released from the House of Detention. The same open and secret traitors saw to it that he was placed under complete prohibition from writing. Thus they obtained complete muzzling of his ecclesiastical testimony.

[12] "*Twee Professoren der Kleine Luyden.*" Luyden is an antiquated form of *lieden*, used with favour by Dutch writers to raise memories of the fact that in the glorious history of The Netherlands, the common, little (lower class) people had always been the power of its resistance in faith against tyranny. In this article Rev. Knoop comments upon the grief of the common people regarding Dr. Schilder, and their consternation and shame regarding Dr. Van Schelven's perfidy. —Trans.

[13] "*Geen Kerkstrijd.*" In this long article, taken up in the Appendices of the Dutch original, the author answers Dr. Van der Vaart Smit. When war broke out in The Netherlands this man appeared as member of the staff of a pro-Nazi periodical in which he criticized the Reformed (*Gereformeerd*) Churches for having decided synodically that anyone holding and advocating the principles of the National Socialist Movement (N.S.B.) could not be a member of the Church of Christ. Dr. Van der Vaart Smit asserted in that article that Synod's decision was taken under the driving pressure of Dr. Schilder. Then the article continued to impress that this decision was, of course, in error because the Church does not concern itself with political things. In a lengthy and courageous article Rev. Knoop refutes the claims of this pro-Nazi article. Incidentally, at the time of translating this book (1947) Dr. Van der Vaart Smit was in jail awaiting execution of his sentence as a traitor to the Dutch nation. —Trans.

I meant this as an answer to an article under the same title in the pro-Nazi periodical, *Evangelie en Volk* (Gospel and People). To these two articles the Germans at first did not react. A reaction, however, did appear. For in the bulletin of October 26, 1940, I wrote an article entitled, *Professor Dr. K. Schilder*.[14]

By means of this article, I opposed the rank nonsense of Rev. Van der Vaart Smit, a Reformed (*Gereformeerd*) pastor who, forsaking his post and collaborating with the enemy as a traitor *par excellence* to church and state, had written in September, 1940, about the imprisonment of Dr. Schilder. This rascally, tendentious, slippery, and altogether bad article was not allowed to be left unanswered. Hence, I refuted it, and the results followed. The Germans, whose attention was most probably directed to it by Dr. Van der Vaart Smit, soon reacted to it. In the first half of November 1940, I was summoned to the German Security Police Office at Rotterdam. There I was first questioned with the greatest pretended good-will concerning what I had written about the imprisonment of Dr. Schilder. The insincere, clammy friendliness of the Germans has become sufficiently known to us. The Gestapo officer, introducing himself as Simon, was a man with a pronounced criminal face, a degenerate type. He wanted to claim that I had discussed "politics" in my article. The gentleman, as you see, was immediately on his German hobby-horse. I most emphatically denied his suggestion and tried to make plain to him that the involved article was simply a reaction to what Dr. Van der Vaart Smit had first written in *Evangelie en Volk*. I tried to make him see that his presentation of Dr. Schilder's article (and prayer) was altogether beside the

---

[14] This very long article deals with the meaning of a passage of Dr. Schilder in *De Reformatie* which read: "Power and authority are fortunately two different things. Finally the Antichrist will have the one and the Church will maintain the other. And then comes the day of the great harvest. Come, Lord of Harvest, yes, come quickly. Come across the English Channel and across the Brenner Pass, come via Malta and Japan, yes, come from the ends of the earth and bring Thy pruning-knife with Thee, and be gracious to Thy people, for they are wholly competent, but only through Thee, through Thee alone, or Thy eternal good pleasure." Dr. Van der Vaart Smit accused Schilder of seeking martyrdom in the manner of Niemöller and of flatly praying in this passage for England's victory over Germany, and of not keeping his religion unmixed with politics. Rev. Knoop defends this passage as being a highly poetical prayer for the sanctification and salvation of the Church, with no reflection on the course of the war whatsoever. —Trans.

point, and that I had in the bulletin merely straightened out what Dr. Van der Vaart Smit had, consciously and purposely, distorted.

But my defence availed nothing. Dr. Schilder, he insisted, had plainly written about political things, as he regarded it evident from Schilder's article. That was undeniable. And I had taken up his cause and defended him. Hence, I also had written about "political things." And that was forbidden. That should not happen again or measures would be taken against me. When I pointed out to him that *Evangelie en Volk*, the periodical of Van der Vaart Smit, had been allowed to write about "political things" he answered that this periodical was a friendly periodical which had rights and privileges above every periodical which revealed enmity towards the Germans.

He stated nothing about eventual measures against me. On this point he left me in the dark.

I thought the interrogation was ended and rose to go. However, such was not the case, for he suddenly broached the subject of my first two articles. He did not name them, though they lay before him, but he plainly referred to their content. So I had written about church conflict. Altogether unexpectedly, he asked me what I thought about the *so-called German church conflict. And what of Pastor Niemöller*? It was a cleverly laid trap. The gentleman was testing me. But fortunately I saw through him. Watch your step for that trap, I thought to myself. So I answered that at his own word I had been summoned to give account of my article defending Dr. Schilder's passage in *De Reformatie* and that I felt justified in limiting our discussion to that. At the same time I said that naturally I had an opinion about the German church conflict. I purposely omitted his "so-called." He did not enter into my answer, but with a sweet little smile on his fat face began to instruct me about the German church conflict. He told me that there had never been a church conflict in Germany. And, of course, in The Netherlands the people were altogether wrongly informed about it. As concerned Pastor Niemöller, so he said, he was no witness of the faith, nor was he a martyr, but someone who had misused his pastoral office to commit a number of "political" offenses. *And for this he had been punished*. But this had nothing to do with church conflict. (Later this same nicety would be proclaimed by Dr. H.H. Kuyper

36

in *De Heraut* of June 8, 1941.) So I had better bear this in mind: for National Socialism desired no church conflict and would never seek it. And where it held the power, a church conflict would never arise. In The Netherlands that would also never happen under the National Socialist rule. But if some pastor made himself guilty of "political" transgression, that was simply an offence committed against the German state, and was a case of *bringing the German state into danger.* Consequently, the German authorities would not hesitate to mete out appropriate punishment to any pastor who made himself guilty, according to *their* judgment, of a "political" offense.

But, of course, that would not be a church conflict.

Later, in other interrogations, I first came to understand that everything that the Church and its office-bearers, in their testimony according to God's Word, spoke against those Nazi doctrines, which were undermining and destroying the Church and her faith, were simply counted as "political" offenses. Properly speaking, every office-bearer who faithfully fulfilled his God-given office always made himself guilty of a "political" offense, and thus was always liable to punishment. In this manner, the real "church conflict" was deftly and conveniently camouflaged; the conflict which Nazism had carried on from the beginning of its rise and would also carry on in our land against those who were spiritually faithful. And any ecclesiastical victim who fell to its violence would thus be nothing but a "political" victim, never a witness for the faith or a martyr for the cause of Christ and His Church and the Word of God.

This lesson, which I received completely free of charge there at the German Security Police Office, was plainly a reaction to what I myself had written about the church conflict in the bulletin of October 5, 1940. But I still felt duty-bound to say something before I departed. To his profession that the German authorities desired and sought no church conflict, I answered that the Reformed Churches which I served did not either. But I immediately added that if it became necessary, they would surely not avoid that battle. The Calvinistic people, very strongly attached to their liberty as a church, would surely not consider any surrender if it became a question of the free Church and the free proclamation of the Word of the Lord, or when the question would become the competency of the Church and her offices. For she would be more obedient to God than to men. And I added that the Calvinistic people would be willing to make the ultimate sacrifice for this.

In this I was still naive. I over-estimated the Calvinistic element of the nation. Or rather, I did not see how diluted and spineless it had become. Under the "leadership" of those who "led" the Reformed (*Gereformeerd*) Churches and also the General Synod at that time, these Reformed Churches would evade offering up the ultimate supreme sacrifice in the cause of the Lord. For this cause our fathers had once even shed their blood.

Thus my first interrogation, which must have lasted about an hour, was concluded, and I could go.

I was not too badly impressed with the outcome. I asked myself whether some form of punishment would still follow, or whether they would let it go at this intimidation.

Well, punishment did follow. On November 28, 1940, the publisher of the *Delfshavensche Kerkbode* received notice that its publication would be prohibited for an undetermined time. I am thankful to the publisher of this periodical that he had never hesitated to place my articles, even though they could have brought him great financial injury. Through a mistake of the German authorities, this prohibition was lifted in the beginning of May, 1941, and the periodical again appeared on May 10, 1941. However, this did not last long. On October 27, 1941, a second prohibition of the bulletin was issued, which in the meantime had been changed into *Mededelingenblad* (Announcement Sheet). Again I was the guilty cause, for in the issue of September 6, 1941, as the editor for the month, I had written a meditation on Psalm 37:12 under the title, "The Ungodly and the Righteous."[15]

---

[15] This vivid and courageous testimony appeared in an appendix of the original Dutch edition. We consider it worthy of being placed in the narrative. Some details can only be understood by translating the text literally from the Dutch Bible. —Trans.

The Ungodly and the Righteous

The ungodly devises subtle attacks against the righteous.
(Ps. 37:12).

The Psalm from which I have taken these words consists of a series of proverbs which are woven together into one whole. They concern the well-known theme with which faith always finds itself struggling against whenever it comes face to face with reality. This theme is: The lot of the pious and the ungodly. These two are not separated from each other, but live together in the one great world-house. They meet each other everywhere, and that meeting must inevitably result in a clash. There is never peace between the two, but always conflict. This conflict has its high points of intensity and vehemence, which bring to the pious deep points of suffering. And now in those deeper points of suffering the situation sometimes becomes too much for the pious and they ask in their grief, "Does God indeed know, and is there knowledge with the most High?"

And now the poet sings about the Divine Righteousness revealing itself in the blessing which He brings on the righteous and the curse with which He strikes the ungodly. It is his purpose to hereby hold the ethical world-order, without which no faith can live, before his reader. But at the same time he exhorts to patience in the firm conviction and trust on God's righteousness. For the victory does not belong to the godless, but to the LORD who defends the righteous and delivers them from all harm. In His own time and in His own way He does this.

Now in this verse, the ungodly are unveiled to reveal their true appearance. The poet says that their real nature is to devise *attacks* against the righteous; that their entire world of thought is ruled by forging attacks against the children of God. They can do nothing else. For does not the righteous obstruct their path everywhere?

The latter are co-workers of God in this world, and struggle to bring every sphere of life under the dominion of the law of the LORD God. They live in the faith that the earth is the LORD's and the fullness thereof. Therefore they desire to subject all of life on earth under the law of the LORD. In every sphere of life they desire to recognize and apply the law. There is for them not a single *neutral* sphere, and there is, in the strict sense, nothing in life that may be classed as an indifferent thing. In everything God's will enters, and the pious seek the subjection of all things to that will of God. And thus their struggle is against the profaning of life in all of its relationships.

Now the life and world-view of the ungodly is diametrically opposed to this. They do not *recognize* any law of God for their whole life and for all of life. And therefore they set themselves against this striving of the righteous to be steadfast and unmovable, always abounding in the work of the LORD, building the temple of the LORD in connection with all of life and sanctifying it all to the LORD. And now it is granted by the grace of the ungodly that the law of God may at best have dominion over the "soul," if this would be a pleasure to the righteous. But they must beware that it causes no inconvenience to the ungodly. Everything outside of the "soul" must remain free from that will of God. All the rest the ungodly brazenly demand for themselves, to rule over it and to use it according to their own free will. And this simply means conflict between the ungodly and the righteous, for both neither can nor will surrender their view of life and of the world. In that conflict, the ungodly devise *attacks* against the righteous. They cannot live with the righteous under one roof. They cannot tolerate the righteous in their surroundings. The righteous are a continual obsession to the ungodly, an offense. And not only the righteous as individuals, but also the communal group of the righteous. If only the ungodly could rid themselves of those righteous, then the way would be open for building the world according to the law of life of the ungodly.

Now you must carefully note that these are subtle attacks which the ungodly devise against the righteous. This pictures them in their dangerous character. They do not look like attacks, much less like subtle attacks. Seen from the outside, superficially, they cannot be recognized as attacks, but rather the opposite. In their plan and execution they are altogether *smooth and adapted*. It requires the sharp and well-trained eyes of faith to penetrate through the outer appearance and discern their true essence. With their mouth the ungodly smile, but in their eyes burns the fire of hell, which is ready to consume and which reflects the hatred of the heart. With one hand they caress, and in the other they carry a hidden syringe with its slow poison, which they hope to secretly administer to the righteous to infect the energy of their faith for the LORD and His cause in the world. The poison of serpents is under their tongue when they flatter with their lips. They are ruled by only one passion, namely, to render the righteous harmless, at all costs, and to clear the way for themselves in the world.

How thankful we must be for this *unmasking* of the ungodly. We can see the ungodly here in the Word of God, pictured for us by the Holy Spirit, in their true likeness, from head to foot. Oh, how we are *forewarned*. Train your eyes by constant and prayerful study of the Scriptures, that you, as sheep among the wolves, may discern the subtle attacks of the ungodly with whom you must live in the world, and that you may take the proper precautionary measures of faith. Woe to the righteous who think they can conclude a careful covenant with the ungodly, in the imagination that thus they can save themselves and the work of the LORD from destruction. This is a fatal mistake and they are playing an unholy game. Woe to the righteous, who, driven by the desire to secure themselves in safety, hand over to the ungodly one piece after another of the work of the LORD, and permit themselves to be shackled by the ungodly in their life of faith. These righteous betray the cause of the LORD, and surrender themselves and that cause into the hands of the enemy. What a bitter disappointment that must necessarily bring about. Sooner or later they will come to see that they have saved neither themselves nor the cause of the LORD, for the simple reason that they have not seen through the *subtlety* of the attacks. There remains, therefore, for believers as individuals and for any community of believers only one thing to do, and that is to pursue the way of a holy warfare against the ungodly and their subtle attacks. Let them confront the ungodly in the form in which the Scriptures picture them. Let the righteous not be misled to depart from the way the LORD has given. May God help us thereto!

*   *   *

For this meditation I was summoned in October, this time not by the German Security Police, but to Room 10 of the Police Office at the Haagsche Veer.

There, in Room 10, the "political branch" of the police had its seat. Now I would be given into the hands of "fellow-countrymen," those brave hurray-shouters, those cowardly betrayers of our land and people, those characterless flatterers of the enemy, who would not hesitate to submit their fellow-citizens to interrogations for the profit of the enemy and to deliver them into the clutches of the enemy. With deep revulsion for this outfit of traitors, I stepped into Room 10.

The man who was about to question me acted with purring sweetness and was condescendingly friendly and polite. That, at least, he had learned from his pay-master: "You must begin by bringing the accused under the delusion that you have the best of will towards him. If he will only quickly confess, all will be forgiven and forgotten, and the penalty need not cause him any big worry. And after the accused is so down-right foolish to believe in your sweetness and good-will, and lets his tongue run away with him, then you may give free rein to your sadistic passion for seeing torture and pain and suffering." That was the calibre of the individual who was about to question me. He really bore the mark of the beast, namely, well-groomed sadism.

This gentleman stated that he knew me. He knew me from the pulpit. He was a church-going man for the advantage of the coming wrath of the N.S.B.

Indeed, he enjoyed listening to a sermon occasionally here and there, and I had also enjoyed his patronage now and then. Well, this pious and church-going gentleman had evidently, already for several years — even before the war — been on the look-out for prey for the future, naturally following his finely developed predatory instincts. And now he *had* his prey which he had shadowed and stalked all these years. He knew, he said, exactly how I felt about the N.S.B. Of course, that was not hard to find out. I had never in any way covered up my opinion about these ecclesiastical, municipal, and social acrobats. At any event, now that he knew how I felt about the N.S.B., I was relieved from telling him. But now he had, he warbled on in liquid tones, read my meditation, "The

Ungodly and the Righteous," and was simply burning to know what I could have meant by that meditation, or rather whom I had in mind by it. I was on the verge of asking him whether that was any concern of his, but thought it better not to be too rough-shod. That would come soon enough. First I wanted to see how he would squirm and twist to reach his purpose. So I restrained myself and asked in turn whether he did not find that my meaning was very clearly expressed in the article. He answered that, yes, he did find it so plain, that he had concluded that with "those ungodly" I had meant the members of the N.S.B. That was his move. Now I was expected to compliment him on his fine sense of feeling; instead, I countered by asking from what he had concluded that by "those ungodly" were meant the members of the N.S.B. Then he took the role of school-master and all his purring friendliness fell away. He reverted to his true nature. What an intensely cruel face that man had when the friendly little smile was no longer there! "No more stories," he demanded. "You had better come out straight forward with the truth and try no more counter questions. Yes or no!" This was exactly the same method which the General Synod of the Reformed (*Gereformeerd*) Churches would later apply to Dr. Schilder, the method used by those who are afraid of arguments because inwardly they know that they are in the wrong.

I then tried to make plain to him that the Bible speaks of two kinds of people who are designated as the righteous and the ungodly, that those two kinds of people are still in the world today, and that everyone who comes to stand before the mirror of the Word of God must decide whether he sees himself in it as righteous or as ungodly, and that thus every member of the N.S.B. can also find his image in that mirror of the Word of God, devotee though he is of a thoroughly anti-Christian view of life and the world.

The end of the story was that he asked me whether I was ready to make an announcement in an upcoming edition of the bulletin, declaring that in my sketch of the wicked I had not meant the members of the N.S.B. I answered him that I could not see the necessity of such an announcement since the meaning of the meditation was plain enough; that I also considered it superfluous, since it would not be necessary for my readers, for whom it was written, because they understood the meaning perfectly; and further, that it did not concern me what outsiders thought of it, and therefore I was not ready to make such an explanation.

This ended the discussion of this subject. I say of *this* subject, because he then began to fish out of me what I thought about the Germans and about their National Socialism, and especially about the N.S.B. I did not withhold my opinion from him.

The interview was ended. Once more I would have to appear before this pocket-sized inquisitor, and then he would deliver me to the Germans. I did not then know that this moment was so near.

The result of this interview was that our church bulletin was prohibited for the second time, on October 27, 1941.

So much for my press articles and the German and "Dutch" reaction to them.

Let me now relate a few things about the interrogations to which I had to submit because of the things I had said in my *sermons and prayer*. Since my notebook was destroyed in a fire which broke out in the camp at Dachau, I am, alas, unable to name the various dates of the different interrogations, of which there must have been approximately six or eight.

Already in the first interrogation, to which I was subjected because of my sermons and prayer, it became evident that all kinds of expressions and sentences, and also reproductions of my sermons and prayers, had been made known to the German Security Police by a betrayer from my own circle, or probably more than one. On the first occasion I told this to the officer who questioned me. At that time I asked him to name my accusers, because I felt that I, as the accused, had the right to know this. "That is none of your business," he said. "It does not at all concern the person who has reported, but regards the question whether you have indeed said these things and said them in this manner." And this I had to admit. But I accompanied this admission with the protest that I was being submitted to interrogation while the accuser was safely hidden behind the screen, so that I could have no respect for such dealings.

Indeed, I actually cared very little whether I knew the names of my betrayers or not. Whether they lived on this street or that boulevard is all the same to me. I hold no malice against those who betrayed me and who are responsible for my suffering in the concentration camp. I rather pity them that they sank so low. And I know that the word of Scripture always receives its fulfilment, also when it says, " 'Vengeance is Mine, I will repay,' says the LORD." It will be fearful to fall into the hands of that God who judges righteously.

Rom. 12:16-19

However, that I am not far amiss when I express the belief that the betrayal originated in my own circle is evident from an article which appeared in the pro-Nazi periodical, *Evangelie en Volk* (Gospel and People), entitled, "Terrorism Everywhere." The article read as follows:

> The persecution of Christians who see things in a National Socialistic light, or are suspected of such views, continues without let-up. Just recently we had a visit from a policeman and his wife who live in one of our largest cities. Both were members of the Reformed (*Gereformeerd*) Church there.[16] Neither one is member of the National Socialistic Movement. Yet both were placed under discipline by the consistory. What is the motive for this action? There were three motives.[17]
> a. The husband was a member of the Justice Front.
> b. He had also collected funds (as a policeman) for Winter Help (the German relief agency).
> c. The wife agreed with her husband.
>
> Is this not strange? It is not clear if the wife was condemned because of her sympathy for Winter Help or for her husband's membership of the Justice Front.
> Let us assume that the consistory judged both matters as equally sinful. In either case, she also was condemned as a member of Christ's Church on earth as if she was a heathen or a publican.
> The consistory [of Rotterdam-Delfshaven] went beyond what the decisions of the Synod of Amsterdam (1936) required of it.
> What could have been the Church's reason for condemning membership of the Justice Front as a sin against God and Christ, worthy of excommunication and the punishment of hell?

---

[16] They lived in my district of the congregation.

[17] It is obvious that the ecclesiastical church discipline was not based on these motives.

What could have been the reason to condemn his collecting for the Dutch Winter Help (even as part of his occupation as a policeman!) as a clear mark of unbelief and hardening in evil? This ecclesiastical discipline was exercised in the name of Christ. However, to me it seems more to be lying to God and a sin against the Holy Spirit than ecclesiastical discipline. This ecclesiastical discipline was said to be exercised in the name of Christ, but in reality was in the name of Roaring Ryan. And when some authorities finally lock up these servants of Roaring Ryan, in order that they can no longer persecute good Christians by such shameful actions of terror, then this is called persecution of Christians.[18] Imagination is also a form of roaring madness. But — what will become of an ecclesiastical world which is led in this manner?

I know the policeman mentioned in this article, who told these *lies* about his ecclesiastical discipline.

The several interrogations which I had to undergo *for the Word of God and the testimony of Jesus Christ* still fill me with great *joy*. By the merciful providence of my God, I was allowed to direct matters in the interrogations in such a manner that they were not limited to the questions of the German Security Police and my answers. Instead, they gave me the opportunity to witness to the German Security Police of the meaning of the Word of God for all ecclesiastical, municipal, and social life, and the meaning of Jesus Christ the *Kurios*, the Lord of lords, to whose authority every authority in the world is subject, even that of the Third Reich. As long as I was free I had always wished that if I would ever be taken captive it would not be for a slip of the tongue, but *for the Word of God and the testimony of Jesus Christ*. Now, for this cause and for this one alone, I was arrested, even though those who arrested me will call this resistance for the faith "a political offence."

Of course it could not be anything else if you consider that the Church and the ecclesiastical preaching of the Word only apply to matters of the soul and the salvation of man, while all other matters, outside this domain, belong to the domain of the state.

---

[18] This threat was later carried out in my arrest.

Whatever I discussed with the Gestapo officer I can best relate in a summary. I tried to make clear that the meaning of the Lord Jesus Christ and His work is not only a matter of the salvation of mankind but a universal matter. He redeemed the world, life itself. All of life, then, should be brought under the protection and acknowledgement of His Name, and all knees must bow before Him. To Him belong the world, all the kingdoms, and all their glory. He is the highest Authority of all things and by Him and His grace the kings and mighty men of the earth rule. For that reason all creatures must be obedient to His Word. That Word, and *only* that Word, must have dominion in church, in state, and in all of society's relationships. In connection with that, I spoke about the authoritative calling of the Church by Christ, who is her Head, to preach that Word and to declare its authority through the principles revealed in that Word for all spheres of life. I opposed the kind of leadership which National Socialism proposes and practices, which is in essence an assault on the Kingship of Jesus Christ. I spoke about the limits of the authority of the state and about the meaning of Christian action. We also discussed the persecution of the Jews in connection with a sermon. And I spoke against the slow but sure destruction of the Christian press, Christian radio, Christian labour unions, and Christian political parties.

I am very thankful to my God that by His grace I was enabled to speak this testimony of Jesus Christ without wavering.

Certainly, sometimes our discussions became very hot, and once I was tempted to use my hands, for the Gestapo officer was a thorough National Socialist and a heathen. He was a fanatical enemy of Church, Christianity, Jesus Christ, and all spiritual leaders. No trace of Christianity could be observed in him, and I could not move him. Some of the things he insisted on were so terrible and profane, that I had to do my utmost not to lose my self-control. I could clearly see that this was his intention.

The day of my last interrogation was Wednesday, November 19, 1941, which was also the day of my arrest. It was a remarkable interrogation, since it centred around different matters than those I had actually been called for. Therefore I will have to expand on it somewhat. As I mentioned earlier, the German Security Police had received complaints about my prayers prayed from the pulpit, especially about my prayers for our royal family and their return; for our army, navy, and air force; for those who had to suffer in prisons, correctional institutions, and concentration camps; and also especially my prayers for the Jews. I had had to give account several times already; in those accounts I had explained my position on prayer, such as I believed it, after the order of Christ. However, especially *that* I prayed for Her Majesty the Queen, and *what* I prayed for her, the Germans took very ill of me. I understood that the moment was drawing near that they would make an end of it. Their "patience" had lasted long enough, as they told me later.

Before that Wednesday in November, I suddenly had to appear at the office of the German Security Police, on Tuesday, October 28, 1941. I was told that I had to accept a *last word of warning*, and that if they received any more complaints about my sermons and prayers, they would take severe measures against me. The officer did not stop at giving this severe warning; it only served as an introduction in order to intimidate me and to make me flexible for the thunderbolt which was to strike soon. And it struck immediately. *I was given a written notice which said that I promised to no longer pray for the former Queen Wilhelmina, since that would be taken as enmity against Germany.*

They demanded that I immediately place my signature under it. I refused. I then supplied the following motivation for refusing to sign it: first, because I did not acknowledge the qualification "former Queen" since it was not known to me that Her Majesty the Queen had resigned her throne, or that she had been dethroned by a rightful authority. To this first motivation I added a second. At that moment, I realized in what kind of dangerous position I found myself. I saw the danger that the Germans would make a matter which pertained to *the whole Church* into a matter which only pertained to *a certain person*, a matter which concerned only *me personally*. I realized I would soon disappear behind a prison door because, according to them, I had abused my office by drawing *political matters* into the prayers I prayed from the pulpit. I would then be imprisoned for a "political transgression." I realized that this was the danger I was in at the moment. What was I to do? Indeed, the prayer, "for all those who are placed in high places," which is sent up to God every Sunday by the minister of the Word is not a private affair, but an ecclesiastical prayer which the preacher has been ordered to pray by the consistory, and the consistory has been ordered to do so by the King of the Church, Jesus Christ, who commanded it thus in His Word. In this manner I had to try to present my defence.

I clearly remembered that the Gestapo officer during the first interrogation, about a year earlier, had talked about the church conflict. Already then I noticed that what we would call "church conflict" would mean for them "political offence." I realized that the Gestapo officer wanted to apply this type of tactic now too. He wanted to avoid a conflict with the Church about the matter of prayers and their contents by accusing me personally of a political crime. Was it not indeed clear from the written notice which I had to sign, that praying for the former queen would be seen as enmity against Germany, an attack on the state? Well, then, in this manner they avoided the *appearance* of dealing with the Church. "National Socialism," they had claimed, "does not want a church conflict, and will take care that under its dominion there never will be a church conflict." How would it take care of that? By simply isolating the pastor from his church and declaring him guilty of a political offence.

This manner of dealing had not only the great advantage of not coming into conflict with the Church, since only a very impetuous and unwise pastor would have to pay for this transgression, but also the second advantage of intimidating other pastors. Since it was a political offense to pray for the queen, ministers would be doubly careful to weigh the consequences before praying for the queen, since it was a political offence. Thus the sword would cut both ways.

The whole setup then was to keep the matter *personal*! Added to this was the fact that the word "political" could only be interpreted by the Nazis. Others simply had to accept that interpretation. ✳

For the outside world it would be quite clear: It was their own fault that those impetuous pastors ended up in a concentration camp. Thus the Nazis kept their hands clean and did not cause any church conflict. And their propaganda completed the matter. The tool of that great liar, Joseph Goebbels, worked perfectly.

So what was I to do now? I wanted to clear this whole thing from the personal element and have it established as an outstanding matter of the Church, so that any censure against it would mean "church conflict" since the pulpit would then fall under the control of the Nazis. Therefore I expressed my second motivation, "Besides, I may not sign this declaration since I have no authority to do so. You must not come to me; you must go to my consistory. They gave me a mandate to pray for our queen, since they in turn were given a mandate by Jesus Christ, the King of His Church, in His Word. So you are at the wrong address when you appeal to me."

My only concern now was to work out a plan by which I could postpone the inevitable, if only for a few days; then perhaps I could draw my consistory into the case. I would then, first of all, have to make this affair pending with the consistory, and manage to get a declaration which I could use against the German Security Police. My consistory would have to report the case before the Deputies for Correspondence with the [occupying] Government, who could then get into the action by making known to the occupying power the Scriptural perception concerning the prayer for the queen and her royal house. At the same time, these deputies could then refuse any interference of the state into affairs which belong exclusively to the Church, of which Christ is King.

Therefore I asked for time to consider, not because I hesitated to persevere in my denial, but because I now desired to see the entire church brought into the case. And wonder above wonders, I received a few days of postponement. If they had known the purpose for which I had asked they would surely never have granted it to me.

On the evening of that day some people gathered together at my house, among them my colleagues of that time and Dr. Klaas Schilder. During that meeting a declaration was framed. The next evening there was a meeting on short notice of the Consistory of the Reformed (*Gereformeerd*) Church of Rotterdam-Delfshaven, and the declaration was adopted by an unanimous vote.[19]

Thus there was now an official declaration from my consistory to the German Security Police, stating that the petitions on behalf

---

[19] We print this interesting and instructive declaration, found as an appendix in the Dutch edition, here in a footnote:

of the queen were not a personal fad of mine. And the consistory placed itself squarely behind me.

In that same special meeting of the consistory it was decided to make this matter known to the above-mentioned Deputies for Correspondence with the Government, of which Dr. H.H. Kuyper was still chairman. At the same time, the consistory appointed a

---

Rotterdam West, October 29, 1941

In connection with the notice served to me by an official of the German Security Police of Rotterdam, October 28, [1941], according to which stern measures would be taken with me in case I should offer prayer for Her Majesty the Queen in capacity of minister in the public worship service in the Reformed (*Gereformeerd*) Church of Rotterdam-Delfshaven, and in answer to the request directed to me by this official that I should subscribe with my signature to a declaration pertaining to this material,

I, Rev. H. Knoop, Minister of the Word in the Reformed (*Gereformeerd*) Church of Rotterdam-Delfshaven, inform you, having consulted with my consistory, that I cannot sign the above mentioned declaration on the following-grounds:

a) The official who communicated the above to me stated at the time that it involved a prohibition to such a prayer. It is true that later he revoked this statement, but this did not at all take away the indefiniteness that thus arose concerning the scope of the implications involved in such a signing on my part. Now in cases of indefiniteness, it is surely not advisable to give one's signature. And in the particular case of myself, in my capacity as a Minister of the Word who stands under the supervision of the consistory, such a signing was the more inadvisable, since a copy of the declaration submitted to me for signature was denied me. Since I consider such a copy essential, because this declaration concerns a permanent element in public worship in which the consistory takes the lead so that I am responsible to the consistory and must negotiate with it, it is already, for that reason, not permissible to sign a formula which concerns the liturgical prayers and makes decisions concerning them.

b) The matter of public prayer on behalf of the government is not an affair of myself personally, but has regard to the consistory, and therefore sustains connections for its congregation with all the Reformed (*Gereformeerd*) Churches in The Netherlands (and overseas territories), and thus all of these churches collectively.

c) These churches are officially known by the government; they have officially placed in the hands of the government copies of their Church Order and Confessional Standards, and likewise are represented by the government through Deputies for Correspondence with the Government. And since the matter which has been discussed with me concerns the churches as a whole, I would be transgressing proper ecclesiastical order if I made a private and incidental decision in this case.

d) As regards the public prayer on behalf of the government, the Reformed (*Gereformeerd*) Churches, who, indeed, would never willingly transgress the fitting order of things, consider themselves bound by the prevailing law, and therefore also by the provisions which concern a populace living in an occupied territory, as these are fixed in the Regulations for Land Warfare of The Hague, in which regulations the lawful government is distinguished from the occupying power.

committee to gain personal contact with the secretary of the Board of Deputies. This contact was actually also made, and it aroused great hopes. I had no doubt that "my case" would be taken over by these gentlemen. The secretary was wholly in favour of it and

e) In Article 28 of our Church Order, to which all of our churches have bound themselves, the duties of the "ministers, elders, and deacons" towards the government are defined. To this also the undersigned is bound with and through his consistory.

f) This same principle holds for the Synodical decisions taken in regard to the present matter.

g) In Article 36 of the Belgic Confession, which is an agreement of communion for all the Reformed (*Gereformeerd*) churches at home and in the overseas territories, prayer on behalf of the government is officially prescribed. According to our accepted Church Order, no local church or pastor has the right to withdraw himself from that on his own.

h) The same is true of the liturgical prayers which are officially recognized and which also contain prayers to be prayed in official capacity on behalf of the government.

i) All of these supplications rest on the Scriptural command as given, among other places, in 1 Tim. 2:1, 2.

j) The Reformed (*Gereformeerd*) Churches have in their history, already in the preceding century, repeatedly made public profession of the fact (even as they have in very deed maintained this confession and its consequences) that, in the internal ecclesiastical life, the rule maintains that Christ's Kingship over His Church binds the conscience, and that every government or power lacks the authority to interfere with that ecclesiastical life to such an extent that her prescription would bring the Church into conflict with the clear mandate of her King, Jesus Christ. Since then prayer on behalf of the government in the life of the Church is regarded as a concrete act of obedience to the command of Christ, the undersigned does not have the right in this respect to give and to follow on his own initiative another interpretation. For these various elements, the official documents of the Secession (*Afscheiding*) and Doleantie, respectively occurring in the years 1834 and 1886, may be referred to.

(Signed) Rev. H. Knoop

We, the undersigned persons, together constituting the officers of the consistory of the Reformed (*Gereformeerd*) Church at Rotterdam-Delfshaven, declare herewith in the name of the above consistory, that they have read the above declaration of their fellow-consistory member, Rev. H. Knoop, and they declare to acknowledge that the sentiments expressed therein regarding the officially binding relationship of a minister of the Word to the existent ecclesiastical regulations and agreements of ecclesiastical fellowship are the common sentiment of the Reformed (*Gereformeerd*) Churches in The Netherlands.

(Signed) Rev. M. Van Wijk, Chairman
(Signed) A. Fennema, Clerk
(Signed) Rev. J. G. Adema
(Signed) Rev. P. Veenhuizen

was even glad that he was at last able to lay hands on a fact in which the interference of the Germans in the internal affairs of the Church might be fully seen, so that the Deputies for Correspondence with the Government might put up opposition to it. So the secretary informed Rev. Gravemeyer by telephone.

But how bitterly disappointing was the answer which he sent a few days later on behalf of the deputies. The answer read as follows:

The Hague, November 11, 1941

Rev. H. Knoop, Pastor of the Reformed (*Gereformeerd*) Church at Rotterdam-Delfshaven.

Esteemed Rev. Knoop:

Your question of whether it would be desirable to send a copy of the memorandum, which you submitted to the German Security Police, to the various consistories was taken into discussion. Although the consistory of Rotterdam-Delfshaven has the freedom to do this, nevertheless we consider it unwise to do so at this time. Although no certainty exists as to whether the action taken against you was of an incidental character or whether it was the beginning of a progressive action, the first may most probably be assumed to be the case. In that case, the sending of copies to all other consistories would be less desirable. Moreover, the fact that they would not have a copy of the declaration submitted to you for signature would also make the material incomplete. The question involved will be under further discussion.

Sincerely,

In your service,
(Signed) W. Van Dijk.

(*With a pencil the following note was added to the bottom of the letter*:)
It is desirable that you send a few copies to Professor Kuyper, the Chairman of the Board of Deputies [and Dr. Kuyper's address].

Now this answer nicely helped the Germans with their game. The deputies simply passed the buck. What did it matter whether or not the action against me was of an incidental character? Nevertheless, the fact was that the occupying power had interfered in the internal life of the Church, and the Nazi state had taken the pulpit under its control. They asked, perhaps only mine? Of course, only mine. Was this not the obvious way for the Nazis to avoid the appearance of a church conflict? Yet was one interference in one local church not sufficient to make interference a fact? "An incidental case," they said. Yes, indeed, but, nevertheless, an attack on the freedom of the preaching. But the deputies simply passed off the issue with, "It is not evident whether or not this is the beginning of a sustained process of action." That is, "We will wait and see, when this calf has been drowned, whether there are still more calves destined for drowning. After that we can once more talk about the problem that is involved here." But was it a problem? In my simplicity I thought it would not be a problem to pray for Her Majesty the Queen in the Reformed (*Gereformeerd*) Churches, and that it was indisputable that we could not permit the state to interfere with the church. Do we see here the influence or the victory of the pro-German Dr. H.H. Kuyper? I wonder.

However that may be, just as the consistory of Rotterdam-Delfshaven had declared in its statement that prayer is a matter of the Church and that the state must keep its hands off it, so these deputies were duty-bound to tell the occupying power — regardless of whether this was the beginning of a continued process — in the name of the King of His Church whom we must obey rather than men, "Hands off the Church; otherwise church conflict."

But instead of revealing a manly Christian courage, these deputies passed off their duty with a mere silencer, and rather *made me the sacrifice*. Surely, that is plain enough. "The question involved will be further discussed."

This question would be discussed further — after I had safely been locked up in a prison or a concentration camp. How many of these incidental cases would have to occur before it would be plain to these deputies that it was indeed a progressive action? Two, three, or twenty? Would the case then definitely receive a decision? Has the case ever been decided? I have never heard if it has been.

And what about my consistory? Fortunately my consistory had still decided (herein departing from the "advice" of the deputies) to send a copy of the declaration to the German Security Police, to each consistory of the Reformed (*Gereformeerd*) Churches, so that if their pastors would be called to account in a similar situation, they would have time to prepare their answer and would all be able to answer identically, in order to show a united front. Whether my consistory was able to carry out the decision to send these copies I do not know. At all events, my attempt to move the whole Church to stand for her freedom with respect to her prayers met with failure, also because of the unjustifiable attitude of the Deputies for Correspondence with the Government. And so there was nothing left but for me to bear the burden of my obedience to the calling of Christ alone.

Well, I brought the declaration of my consistory to the German Security Police. And I added that I would *maintain* my decision to refuse any promise not to pray for Her Majesty the Queen; also that my consistory had instructed me to answer in this manner, and that the motivation for the answer would be found in the declaration.

Thus I could depart and await the outcome of all this. Would it, perhaps, still avail somewhat? Then something remarkable happened. Not quite as soon as I had expected, but about a week later I was suddenly summoned. And to my surprise I was not summoned to the German Security Police, but to the "political division" of the [Dutch] Rotterdam Police. Having arrived at the Police Office, it soon became evident that I was to be subjected to an examination by the same gentleman who had examined me for my article in the bulletin. Now it would be about a sermon I had preached on October 26, 1941 (note the date, October 26), on Daniel 3:16-18.

I was notified that the "political division" considered it necessary to place me under surveillance. For that purpose they had sent a stenographer to take records of my sermons. They would read the record and allow me to make remarks and corrections. But first I had to answer a few questions.

Did I admit to having preached on that text that day? I confirmed that. Why had I chosen to sing those particular Psalms? I answered him that according to custom I had chosen them as very suitable to the message of the sermon. This he recorded.

Then he began to read the sermon. I must confess that I never heard such a miserable stenographic report of a sermon. Or rather, it was simply a smooth falsification. Therefore I told him that I could not accept this as a true report.

To my surprise, the gentleman took no offense to this at all — indeed, he was an extremely friendly gentleman. All I had to do was to suggest the necessary changes, and he would see that the corrections were made in the final copy. He indeed jotted down my suggested corrections and he read the whole thing once more at the end of our conference, to make sure that no mistakes were possible.

Indeed, he crowned his friendliness by promising me, unasked, that as soon as it was corrected, he would send me a copy so that I could be assured of the corrections.

Now, why all this friendliness?

Was the gentleman's conscience burdened and uneasy because of what he knew was in store for me? Or was it pure comedy and a false promise? Pure make-believe, of course. At the time of writing this, three years after the event, they must still be busy with those corrections. At least I never saw them. But doubtless, he never kept his promise to me.

At that moment it was a riddle to me why that sermon should suddenly bring me into the hands of the Dutch Police, whereas formerly it was the German Security Police. But that riddle was soon solved. It was solved on Wednesday, November 19, [1941] the day of my arrest. Then I suddenly realized that this whole interrogation by the Dutch Police had been a shrewd counterstroke of the Germans, by which they tried, in an unnoticed way, to get rid of that dangerous question of praying for the queen. When I was called before the German Security Police on November 19, I had no other thought but that this would be concerning our declaration which answered their ultimatum about praying for the queen. But I was mistaken. The first thing I heard was, "So, *after the last warning* of October 28, you have again dealt with politics from the pulpit."

I stood amazed. I asked myself what this could mean. For really, I was conscious of not the slightest wrong on my part. And then he came forward with that sermon on Dan. 3:16-18 about which I had been questioned by the Political Department of the Dutch Police, and of which I was still expecting a copy. But (note the date) I had preached it on October 26th. They were evidently afraid of the subject of the General Petition for the Queen. For they had seen through my attempt to make this a case involving all the churches. When I mentioned that we were still to discuss that declaration, he became vehement and said that praying for the queen was of no concern to them at all, we could pray for her as much as we desired, since she would never come back anyway.

When I replied to this false prophesy, "Neither you nor I can know that — God only knows," he laughed sarcastically.

That was my second defeat. The first I suffered at the hands of the Deputies for Correspondence with the Government, who left me to my fate. The second by the Germans who gained a victory by avoiding the real issue. They no longer had any interest in the matter regarding praying for the queen, but I could see that they were very much interested in me personally. Then began the most unedified discussion that I ever had with the German Security Police. It was fortunately the last. It was about that sermon on Daniel. My questioner repeated that I had dared, after the last warning, nevertheless to bring my politics on the pulpit. I asked him to state when that sermon was preached. After a little search he answered, "*October 26.*" Then I asked, though I myself well knew, when they had last given me that warning. Also this the papers showed: "*October 28.*" Then I pointed out to him that the accusation of preaching "politics" after being warned did not hold *because the last warning was given two days after this sermon was preached*.

He hesitated. Why? Had these dates escaped him?

Of course not. Rather, it seemed that he was awaiting a proposal from me.

I waited. I waited to see whether he would still dare to arrest me, even after he had declared the affair of praying for the queen as finished, and after his accusation of preaching "politics" *after* the warning had proven ungrounded.

He did dare. "For," he said, "*you are plainly inclined that way.*" And I admitted it, even though in a totally different sense than he meant. He meant inclined to political offense; I meant inclined by faith to obey and fight for the Word and the cause of the Lord.

And then that sermon. My lot was plainly decided, but for the sake of procedure, certain legal grounds had to be established in order to arrest me. Hence the sermon from Daniel was brought to the fore. Its theme was:

The Confessing Church maintains her resistance for the faith against the demands of a world-power regarding her national religion:
  1. By refusing to acknowledge the need of self-justification
  2. By confessing the perseverance of religious faithfulness

The discussion which followed about the sermon was very unpleasant. The gentleman was in a bad mood and easily provoked. His mask of simulated German friendship was now wholly gone. The brute barbarian appeared in full array. He threatened, leaped up, and as one possessed, came towards me with clenched fists as if to strike me in the face, shrieked hysterically, and suddenly became as sweet as a kitten. But thanks be to God, it did not avail him. I remained unmoved, and he could not inspire me with terror, nor make me pliable. Psalm 46 stood clearly before my mind: "God is our refuge and strength, a very present help in trouble." I breathed a passionate prayer to that God for strength and grace to be faithful. And it pleased Him to sustain me in that hour and to make me faithful in this lion's den, in order to maintain my testimony for Jesus Christ, the Lord. To Him be all the honour.

During the discussion of the sermon, the hypocrisy and untrustworthiness of the Dutch Nazi who had interrogated me about it in the political department became evident. It had all been pure make-believe. To be sure of their plan, they had put two irons in the fire. Iron No. 1 was the question of praying for the queen, and iron No. 2 was the sermon on Daniel 3. Surely from one or the other they could accomplish their purpose. *For they had plainly settled that I would be arrested*. For Iron No. 2, the sermon, they had collaborated with the Dutch Nazi office. But that Dutch Nazi had known all about it. His interrogation of me was just a little game for the sake of procedure. Of the promised corrections in the stenographic report of the sermon, not one had been made. This slave of the German lords had simply submitted the slovenly, or rather, smoothly corrupted, copy of my sermon to the office of his paymasters, the German Security Police, with not one of the promised corrections made.

When I complained about this neglect to these Germans, I received the very logical answer, "The men of that political department are our friends; you are not. They speak the truth, so you must be lying." Period!

After we had talked for a few more hours about the sermon, and it had once more become evident how I was inclined, they laid the typed report of the case before me to sign as evidence.

The officer picked up the phone and called the prison-van.

Now I knew that my case had come to an end. The preparation for my imprisonment was finished. It was about 1:00 P.M. I was tired. This thing had been going on since about 9:00 A.M.

Beneath the window passed one of my colleagues. Just a moment before he had told the Gestapo officer that he had warned me to ease up on that kind of preaching.

Half an hour later, I was at the office of the Dutch Nazis on the Haagsche Veer, and after routine details were taken care of, I was locked up in cell 25.

"A theatre in Dachau" had its beginning in this prelude.

5. Reactions in My Own Circle

It need surprise no one that my activities from May 14, 1940 until the day of my arrest (November 19, 1941) called forth the most contrasting reactions in our circle. This is a common occurrence in such cases. I would say no more about it, except that in our Reformed (*Gereformeerd*) circle the contrasts that would later appear so sharply were already beginning to manifest themselves in my surroundings.

I was also bothered by the realization that very few understood the true meaning of my activities and efforts. Very few understood that I was carrying on a struggle of principles and that my resistance was one of faith for the sake of my church, country, and people.

Those few who lived close to the Scriptures had an eye open for the grave dangers with which the Church and Christian life and action were treated by the infiltration of the Nazi principles. Their living in trust by the Word of God gave them an open eye for the fact that very subtle assaults were being undertaken against the Church, the life of the Christians, and everything which was built on the principles of Scripture. These few clearly saw through the words and deeds of the Nazis, no matter how carefully they were camouflaged. They discerned with shock and offense that their most prized institutions were slowly but surely being broken down.

They agreed with me that resistance for the faith against these subtle attempts was imperative, no matter what the cost, since nothing less than their most precious possessions were at stake. Fired by the same ideals, they prayerfully fought together with me in the battle. As long as I live I will continue to be thankful for the powerful spiritual support which those faithful brothers and sisters lent me. Belonging mostly to the common folk, Calvinism continued to live in these people in its purity. It appeared that the hardy race of the "little people" (kleine luyden) had not yet died out.

Among these all, I remember with special gratitude the faithful brethren of my own pastoral district, Section D. They always stood by me and encouraged me even though they were often filled with care and anxiety for my safety. They understood. They demonstrated this without any unnecessary words. It was such a help in that grave struggle, more, perhaps, than they surmised or than I could let them feel. How deeply, how warmly, how faithfully they lived along with me and prayed for my struggle, when I would again be summoned to give account for my stand. How they filled "the lonely vigil of the watchman" with the fellowship of their love and faith.

However, not all were as faithful as some of these "little people." Some made my cause very heavy to bear by their wrong understanding of my actual intentions, or by taking out on me their lack of necessary faithful courage in peevish spite or insinuations. I was at least able to appreciate those who discussed the situation with me and expressed their dissatisfaction with me. At least these were open and aboveboard. But I had grave objections to those who did not direct their objections to me, but to others behind my back; from them I experienced great grief. They were the back-biters who betrayed the Lord's cause.

There were those who openly told me that, according to their estimation, I was playing a dangerous game, dangerous for the Church and for myself: I was risking my life, and they had no appreciation for this. They advocated the "caution" which in those days was a prime requisite. The wisdom (caution) of serpents apparently interested them more than the uprightness of doves. And of this caution of serpents they had an understanding that fit all to well into their game. Its purpose was to save one's life at whatever cost, even surrendering one principle after another to accomplish this. Here we see an attitude of life which, to my mind, is in diametric conflict with the first principles of the Gospel. Already here one can see the lines of spiritual decay which would later increase in such a dreadful manner.

However, there were others among this group who called themselves Christians, who fostered a growing mentality which later became the ruling attitude towards the invader and his demands — parallel to that which appeared in other groups in our country. This mentality can, perhaps, best be characterized as a lack of Christian manliness; worldly calculation and faithlessness to and betrayal of principles for which they had once contended, when it was not dangerous and required no sacrifice of life. They were the ones who did not dare to lose their lives. They were also the ones who withdrew and shortened their spiritual battle-front without a blush, simply accepting the destruction of the Christian system of principles with fatalistic shrugs of the shoulders, in order to enjoy repose.

Both of these classes made eager use of that suddenly popular text concerning the caution of serpents. I immediately discerned in them that easy but dangerous quoting of the Scriptures according to mere sound. That is sinful and a violation of the Scriptures.

To warn against this, I wrote a meditation on that text in our church bulletin.[20]

---

[20] This article also appeared in an appendix in the Dutch edition. We have translated the text literally from the Dutch Bible and inserted it here in the narrative. —Editor.

The Caution of Serpents and Uprightness of Doves

Therefore, be cautious as serpents and upright as doves.
(Matt. 10:16)

It is undeniable that in certain times and situations, men take the occasion to work with certain Bible texts. That almost works as an epidemic. They become mottos which pass from mouth to mouth and remain in style as long as the particular situation lasts, but as soon as the situation passes by, these texts pass into the realm of the forgotten.

Also the above-quoted text is at present enjoying this questionable honour. However, one cannot avoid the impression that it is being quoted very arbitrarily, according to the mere sound of the words, so that the passage is really violently abused and torn out of its context. This always happens when one uses a text "loosely." Besides this, the accent is usually on the first part of the text. With a wink which says, "You know what I mean," they say, "Be wise (cautious) as serpents." That is, be slippery and shrewd and know all the loop-holes. Then the second part of the text trails behind like a lame horse; it is an item which is simply repeated out of mere habit. Serpents and doves — especially serpents — have become very popular animals, in their particular mode of life as creatures, by the peculiar situation in which we find ourselves as a church.

Now we must first of all remark that the circumstances in which we find ourselves as confessing Christians, bring with them the danger of being misled. Against this being misled, the confessor of Christ must offer resistance for the Word of God. The temptations of today are especially designed to weaken our confession of the absolute Lordship of our Lord Jesus Christ over our life, and to withdraw one principle after another in the sphere of public life from His Sovereign dominion. Christ and the soul, oh indeed, that still has some meaning; but Christ and all human life, that is stretching things too far! The deception is often very subtle and comes in a garb in which it is difficult to be discerned; its constitution is very clever. And so *every* confessor of Christ is called to test the spirits, whether they be of God. Let him whet his sword to join in the fierce spiritual battle in an open fight.

But we must know how this should be done; then we can learn from this text.

Secondly, let us also determine what the true meaning of the word *Christian* is. Then we will learn that it means exactly the opposite of what many mean by it.

In Matthew 10 is recorded the sending of the twelve with the assignment to preach the coming of the Kingdom of God in the land of the Jews. They also received the power to cast out unclean spirits and to heal the sick. Besides prescribing the manner of their activity, the Saviour also pictures for them their future circumstances in this world and the circumstances of all confessors of the Name of Jesus. They will be as *sheep in the midst of wolves.*

Indeed, that is not a pleasant situation. Wolves are not exactly the most enjoyable kind of animals. Rather, they are dangerous, bloodthirsty, and greedy for prey. Especially when they are in packs, as they usually are, the watchword is, "Beware!" And now, into that dangerous situation of life, the confessors of Christ and His Gospel are sent into the world. They must reckon with this grim danger. And this is exactly what they do when they are as cautious as serpents and as upright as doves.

So you will immediately understand the text. Now you can see that this "caution" cannot mean that we must in any form soft-pedal or adjust the confession of Christ to suit circumstances; nor must we make this confession less clear and positive and change it with the circumstances, merely because of a situation that is dangerous for our life as a church or as a Christian. Far from it! That confession must *always*, under *all* circumstances, be absolutely clear and positive. No danger in life ever justifies watering down the testimony that Christ is Lord over our whole life — over *all* of life. The word "cautious" in the text means exactly that every one who confesses Jesus Christ and acknowledges Him as Lord indeed must take very careful account of the condition in which he lives because of this confession. But just as a serpent in danger reveals a wide-awake presence of mind, is fully on guard and alert to everything that looks suspicious, does not carelessly venture without inspecting and discerning its surroundings carefully, and will not for a moment be caught off guard or misled, thus also the Church and believers must live and move in the midst of the wolves.

Thus we must also live and move in our day as among wolves. Our surroundings are hostile. It is a world with spiritual wickedness in the air. This world approaches the Christian with the temptation to weaken the confession of Christ and threatens us with dire consequences if we do not. In opposition to this, we must now stand our ground and not let ourselves be moved even an inch from the stand we have taken, and we must carefully note what dangerous temptations are threatening us. Let that be our "caution." This caution will lead us to the highest activity in word and deed: persevering through faith in the face of dangerous temptations and life-threats, in order to remain in the faith, to stand unmovably firm, not yielding an inch; persevering to confess the absolute Lordship of Christ over all of human life and living.

But in that faith we must, at the same time, be as upright as doves. Being upright in our purposes as confessors of Christ means that we will have no ulterior motives. Our sole purpose is to confess Him, and we do that as innocently as doves. Then we will have nothing secretive, nothing stealthy.

There is nothing that injures or destroys life in this; on the contrary, it advances all that is good for life. There is nothing dangerous for Church or for state, or for life itself in this. By this we really bring a blessing to life, which all may know of, since we are open and aboveboard. Nothing is kept hidden or secret, all is transparent. We are upright as doves.

This text also contains a piece of instruction for our time. Never may we weaken the confession of the sole Lordship of Christ or make it vague. We must, with eyes open for the dangers that are truly threatening, never turn aside from the way on which He has called us to bear that testimony, but we must persevere even though the wolves may threaten. We must do that uprightly and devoutly.

When we do this, we will surely not enjoy ease in this world, but we are not here for our "comfort," but are sent as sheep among the wolves.

Thus we will be a blessing to life, more than we can surmise. Only they who by faith have the combination — the combination of the caution of serpents and the uprightness of doves — bring blessing to life.

*   *   *

This meditation was printed in our church bulletin of October 12, 1941.

There was also another group that acted with covert expressions. Apparently they used the principle, "Half a word to the wise is sufficient." They disapproved of my conduct and let me feel this by way of covert reflections.

Thus I recall — as one of many examples — an elder abusing his prayer, offered for me in the consistory room before I was to ascend the pulpit, in order to give me a hidden warning. He quoted in his prayer the well-known rhymed stanza of Psalm 141:

> *Set Thou a guard, O LORD, I pray Thee,*
> *To keep my mouth from evil's lure,*
> *The doorway of my lips secure.*
> *Hear Thou my voice and come to stay me.*[21]

I cannot doubt but that he meant well, but it was certainly not very appropriate, and, despite all his good intentions, he was misusing Scripture. This Psalm does not deal with loose speech in general, but with the sin of praying without submission to the discipline of the Word. The elder was not justified in using this prayer, which the Psalmist wrote to maintain a well-disciplined approach to God, to give me a hidden warning to be careful with my words on the pulpit. And it was not very manly.

However, I was most deeply grieved by those who passed a hard and unmerciful judgment upon my actions behind my back. They were those who only knew *fear*; colleagues, who from fear — though they claimed other motives — even omitted the petition for Her Majesty the Queen. They desired, if you please, not to provoke the Germans, but at the same time they took out on me

---

[21] Psalm 141:2 (*Book of Praise, Anglo-Genevan Psalter*).

their guilt over their lack of spiritual courage and obedience by strongly condemning my actions to others.

With perfect calmness, they characterized my action as bravado, as soliciting a self-chosen martyrdom, among similar niceties. But they themselves did not dare lift a finger to maintain the holy principles worth our life-blood, for which they had "fought" in the front ranks before May 14, 1940; then it did not require a single sacrifice, at least not the sacrifice of their lives.

They were the deserters. To them we may apply the lines of the *Geuzen Liedboek 1940-1945*,[22] which describe them as traitors, cowards, cads, rascals without courage, breakers of vows who think only of themselves, and are not inclined to make any sacrifice whatever for their country — an offense to the true patriot!

These men indeed caused a great deal of mischief and much harm to the cause of Christ, and they occasioned the by-standing enemy a great amount of jovial pleasure. Between them and myself lie the bodies of my colleagues who were murdered in Dachau: the Reverends Sietsma, Kapteyn, and Tunderman. Alas, how little understanding there was of the *prophetic task* in the ministry of the Word, and of the calling to account of the watchman on Zion's walls. How small a grasp the Word of God seemed to have on the hearts of people unto an obedience of faith, which pays attention to the commandment and is blind for the consequences. How spiritually poor we were and how deformed our church and spiritual life were! Where did we hear the ringing voices and see the deeds of our "old heroes?" Few were gripped by the motto, "For Zion's sake I will not hold my peace." It was by the grace of God alone, and nothing else that I was able to resist the influence of this negative reaction and not be withheld from my purpose. My life in those days was one great antithesis in the tension for and on behalf of the message of the Word of God which I was bound to bring. This necessity was laid on me. How can I possibly explain to others what that was? To understand it one must himself have been in that situation.

---

[22] Beggar's Song Book. In the tradition of the so-called (sea) beggars of the Eighty-Years-War, who fought for the Dutch independence from Spain. This particular song, of which Rev. Knoop quoted the first seven lines in the Dutch edition, was written by G.C. Snyder. —Editor.

In short, it was not being able nor willing to do otherwise. It was a matter of, "I must; God wills it, and I cannot do otherwise. May *He* help me." Moreover, I was deeply convinced that it was not because of *me*. God did not need me. I was simply required to be willing to lose everything — freedom, even life itself. That is not pleasant, indeed. The great and holy cause of the Lord was involved. It was this, this cause alone I desired to serve, and nothing else. I was concerned that the people of God would remain steadfast and immovable, always abounding in the work of the Lord; also, no, *rather*, because of the precarious position in which the people became involved by the occupation of our country. No price was too costly for this, since it concerned the rights of our people, whom I loved and who were oppressed and exhausted by a cruel tyrant, and this involved the justice of God. To stand for the justice of God is our high calling. No sacrifice is too great for that cause.

All of this had taken hold of me, drove me, and continued to drive me to say what, according to my inmost conviction, God required me to say in spite of the impending reaction of my own circle, according to the words of our National Anthem:

> *That I may stay a pious*
> *Servant of Thine for aye.*

And having received help from God, I persevered unto the end.

6. The Tragedy of the "Leaders"

The well-known Czech statesman Masaryk was asked by a journalist, upon receiving word that he had been appointed president of Czechoslovakia, whether or not he was happy with the distinction. "Happy?" he answered. "No, I am not happy, but I have a feeling that we may not be disappointing." That is the language of one who is not ambitious for a political plume or a post of honour, but is deeply conscious of his great calling and is, therefore, fully conscious of his great responsibility. Being a true leader is a matter of great responsibility, which one must assume with its most dire consequences, and therefore is at the same time a matter of sacrifice. True leadership means being a devotee, sacrificing that which is most precious and dear. A leader lives solely for those whom he must lead. To him the words of Brand apply:

> *Though you should offer all but life,*
> *Your sacrifice is nothing still.*

He who is called to be a leader and is not ready to accept the extreme consequences had better not accept the task. He is nothing more than a disappointing jumping-jack, not fit for the task. He is a despicable seeker of sinecures who toys with duty and gambles with his appointed trust for the sake of personal advantage, gain, and glory. He is a filthy bankrupt who should be brought to justice for swindling. He does not care at all if he causes disappointment.

How glorious it would have been, and how significant and different, if all those who were called to leadership in the Reformed (*Gereformeerd*) Churches, in any sphere of life, had given evidence of such a deep consciousness of their calling during the German occupation! Instead, a disturbing lack of leadership came to light. Ability and character did not prove able to cover each other. Again, as of old, it was the "little people" who stood immovable, while many who had such preeminence over the "little people" either simply toppled over, quickly got off their leader's seats, or tried, by shifting and fitting, by yielding step by step, to save their own little affairs. Or else they were conspicuously absent from field or highway. Were not journalists, politicians, preachers, and officers of various organizations duty-bound to give leadership and guidance to the Christian people as it sought for guidance in the great difficulty in which it suddenly found itself?

Surely they had the right to expect every leader to speak up saying, "Here we are, you can depend on us. We are attacking; follow us! Now it is as never before, but you are not alone." This was the fire-test of their principles which showed what they were really worth to us. This was also the fire-test which showed what we were worth. Right now, especially now, we had to live from those principles, whatever the cost. With tact, surely, but also with firmness and stability. *That is how it should have been*. That would have been a feast in the midst of our great sorrow. But did they live up to that expectation? Alas, very many did not. They would have moved mountains if they had possessed faith as a mustard seed. They would have lived up to it if they had lived in the strong consciousness of their calling of responsibility *now*, of self-sacrificing devotion *now*. They would have lived up to it if the principles they preached had been a part of their flesh and blood. But, alas, it appeared that for many this was not the case, and therefore in our own circles we had to behold the *tragedy of the "leaders."* We were witnesses of the desertion of many who were called to be leaders, or at least whom we had always considered as leaders. We discerned the faithlessness and cowardice of many who had climbed to a seat of leadership, and clung to it with a cramped clutch. So we discerned that they did not carry the feeling that they must not cause disappointment.

Oh, how they did cause disappointment, many of those "leaders" who did not prove worthy of this privilege of grace! Did they ever really for one moment foster that inner anxiety which says, "If only we do not cause disappointment." But it was only when there were no clouds in the sky that they were such principled men. Before the war, when the elections were again at hand, they gave deeply principled guidance. They were favourite speakers at mass-meetings. The youth-meetings received their enthusiastic enlightenment. They battled with words, hard words, and witty words, against the principles of the N.S.B., because these conflicted with Scripture. They forcefully called men to battle, to stand for the antithesis. But at that time it was quite easy and brought them no small profit. But when the sky began to turn cloudy, did they offer their freedom, their lives, their position, their honour?

Then God finally deemed it time to purge His threshing floor. When their fire-test in the shape of the German occupation came, where did they stay? What did they do? Were they equal to the test? God blew down all their display and appearance of sufficiency.

Yes, indeed, it was the tragedy of the "leaders."

That was the great offense of which I had to take note for about a year and a half before my imprisonment — an offense which I often mentioned in my preaching. I heard our people complain in great vexation that they had looked to their highly beloved and trusted leaders for guidance, but had been failed by them. I saw their deep consternation when they discovered that the leaders had either disappeared or had begun to negotiate with the enemy, and were trying to save the situation for themselves by the policy of yielding, rather than letting them demolish; or were giving them advice, for example about their treatment of the Jews, which was in diametrical opposition to their previous preaching. Thus people complained that their pastor would not pray for the queen and the lawful government, and if he did, his prayer was so diplomatic that one had to ask, "Now what was he really praying for?" So they tactfully moved away from the truth, lest they came into conflict with the prowling Gestapo. They would not risk their life for Christ and the sake of His Gospel.

One of my colleagues once said to me, "I can still say so much that is glorious about the Lord Jesus," to which I replied, "Then why do you not once mention this glorious fact, namely, that He is *Lord*, and that no man, no *Führer*, is lord besides Him. Is not your official calling to say everything about Him that you find in the Bible?"

There was also constant complaining by Christians concerning their Christian daily periodical, which used to give such vigorous leadership, but now was simply never being forbidden. And why not? Because it twisted itself into every possible shape so that it might maintain its existence. Because it was not faithful, it gradually permitted itself to be assimilated by the German rule, to at last lend itself to the Nazi propaganda in order to help infect our Christian people therewith. This was what *De Standaard* did, their standard, the publication of Abraham Kuyper, who in the past had aroused and led the *Kleine Luyden* (the "little people").

There was constant complaining about church periodicals. How great was the consternation concerning the "leadership" of *De Heraut*, a "leadership" which was definitely pro-German in spirit. It was a vassal which sold itself to the oppressors, thereby being able to preserve its regular size. Meanwhile, well-known professors and ministers continued to lend their cooperation to this Germanized periodical.

There was complaining over the lax leadership given by the Synod of the Reformed (*Gereformeerd*) Churches. Did this Synod really give leadership? Did it give fearless testimony against the constantly expanding, constantly more pervading, ever-further encroaching Nazi terrorism which appeared in the Jewish programs, the imprisonment of pastors, and the labour-camp measures? The Reformed (*Gereformeerd*) Churches do not stand out among the Christian churches for courageous and tenacious resistance for the faith. Later a highly placed Gestapo testified that the Reformed (*Gereformeerd*) Churches were the most pliable.

But this Synod *did* have the courage to persecute brothers and to cast them out in a manner very much akin to the methods practised by Nazism. Those simple Reformed (*Gereformeerd*) people saw this clearly and plainly as well, and they were bitterly grieved by it. *This grief was for the corruption rooted at the centre of the institution.*

Thus they complained in advance about the surrender to the demands of an occupying power which did not honour a single international rule of warfare, even though this power had subscribed itself to it. What about the required "Aryan Declaration?"[23] If the "Christian leadership" had given forceful and courageous advice to say "No!" to this demand — because it was not at all a measure of administration, but entirely an action to prepare for the gruesome and cowardly persecution of the Jews and, ultimately, their eradication — surely much Jewish suffering would have been avoided.

And what did *De Heraut* dare to write about this persecution in the issue of November 17, 1940? Why was the declaration of the Protestant Churches to Seyss Inquart concerning the persecution of the Jews, not read from the Reformed (*Gereformeerd*) pulpits? Why? *De Heraut* answered, "[Because] such an announcement from the pulpit in public worship would endanger those who made the announcement." Why, then? To save one's life. And to save the "life" of "our" churches. As if that was most important. Did they not know that Hitler had said that he would solve the Jewish problem? And did they not know that such a solution meant, in the vocabulary of National Socialism, nothing but annihilation? Or, were they blind though seeing, deaf though interrogation? And could they not know that everyone who signed this declaration became personally responsible for the great misery which soon overcame our Jewish countrymen?

Why did the "leadership" not call for a front of open resistance, a resistance through obedience in faith by all who know that their

---

[23] A census issued to ferret out all Jewish blood. —Trans.

salvation is of the Jews? A massed resistance for the faith could have effected very much. Even if it had not, we would still have had a quiet conscience that we had been faithful to our calling before God with respect to the Jews as well. But the "leadership" failed. Read again what Dr. H.H. Kuyper dared to write in *De Heraut* of December 8, 1940, and you will be filled with deep indignation about what this unfaithful "leader" did not hesitate to bring forth.

I still believe that a massed resistance could have accomplished much. This was seen, for example, in the case of the churches' care for the needy, in which the Germans also wanted to meddle. I myself experienced that if one gave a well-motivated reason, one could very well accomplish something. The same was true with regard to the occupying power, which wanted to centralize and rule everything. It demanded that those who planned to hold a lecture had to inform the authorities in advance of its contents. Thus we simply let ourselves be controlled and muzzled. Several times I refused and informed them to come and listen if they wanted to know. It is better to be prohibited from speaking than to speak while wearing a muzzle. Thus it was with the members of the Department of Culture and others. The "leadership" of the Reformed (*Gereformeerd*) section of our people kept silent and so the people became members of such National Socialist organizations.

Barring a few laudable exceptions, our confessing journalists shied from making the sacrifice for Christ's sake by joining the National Socialistic Fraternity of Journalists, to save their jobs and their lives. But the leadership was silent — or led the way.

It is not surprising that our Reformed (*Gereformeerd*) people, left in the lurch by their leadership, felt forsaken. And, since the leaders erred from the path, the sheep also wandered off. In many cases, the responsibility for the breakdown of the resistance for the faith lay with the leaders. Certainly, how differently our Reformed (*Gereformeerd*) people would have acted if all those who were called to give leadership had all proved true, and if they had confirmed their lofty pre-war words by equally noble deeds. Here the lack of a sense of responsibility became manifest. The instinct to save one's own life was altogether too strong. Oh, indeed, if this had been different, many more victims would have fallen, and many more would have had to undergo the gruesome suffering of the horrible concentration camps. But was not the cause of the Lord worth all this, even apart from the cause of the oppressed and tyrannized fatherland?

This might all have become very dreadful, but one thing is certain: Our Reformed (*Gereformeerd*) people would have been proud of these leaders, and in the event that they came through this conflict alive, would have received them after the liberation of the country with open arms, eager to follow their firm leadership. How mighty and beautiful the flowering of our life of faith would then have been! Alas, this faithlessness has been an abomination to the Lord. It has surely avenged itself.

It was not only complaints about the tragedy of these "leaders" that I heard during the year and a half before my seizure. I also heard something else. "Our people" drew from this tragedy a definite conclusion for the future. They would *never forget* this. For of course, it would not be at all impossible that when all this was past — recall how things went after the Napoleonic occupation — they would see the spectacle of all these deserting leaders coming unashamedly out of their hiding places to sit in the saddle and again take up the reins of leadership. "But," they grimly assured, "they shall not succeed. Whether they are preachers, journalists, burgomasters, legislators, party officials, or labour leaders, they will have to comfort themselves with the fact *that their little kingdom is done for, that they are finished and not needed anymore.* First of all there must be a thorough purging! They may have been ever so capable, but they have proved to have no character. It would just be a little too naive to allow a responsible leader who defaulted in the hour of peril to calmly take up the reins again later. By their laxity they have proved that they were not equal to the calling of confirming their words with deeds, and did not dare do the weighty tasks that the hour demanded." It was this conviction which I saw growing deeper in the people in those days, and in my last interrogation I testified to the German Security Police of this conviction.

The tragedy of the "leaders" is one of the saddest episodes in the history of the occupation.

7. Behind the Closed Door

And so, on November 19, 1941, the door of cell 25 of the police jail on the Haagsche Veer closed behind me. This completed the introduction to the theatre in Dachau.

My stay at this jail, and also at the one in Scheveningen, from November 19, 1941 - April 17, 1942, can best be characterized by these lines:

> *The door is shut*
> *The walls are dumb,*
> *Days and nights spent in a cell.*
> *But Christ can sanctify this hell*
> *To be a heaven-touched sanctum.*

Indeed, it was a sanctuary. When the door of that cell closed behind me on that afternoon, my first thought was, What use can I, in these bonds, be to my church and my people? Have I now become utterly insignificant and worthless? Do not forget that I was placed in solitary confinement and I could not read or write; in fact, all day long all I could do was nothing. I was strictly isolated. I had to wash, shave, bathe, and take fresh air strictly alone. I immediately saw that I must now make use of that mighty means God has given to His children on earth, that power which can accomplish more than the millions of Allied soldiers or the most concentrated bombardments, the power which would finally cause the mighty Third Reich to shake on its foundations and crash in ruins. That means was prayer. In that little cell, the Third Reich had locked up one unimportant man who, if he knew and fulfilled his calling, would be a great danger for that Reich. Oh, indeed, under the permissive guidance of God, the Third Reich had been able to silence my lips in my prophetic office and in the ministry of the Word, but it was not able to stop my priestly activities by this confinement. Christ would change this little cell into a sanctuary in which His *priest*, as *intercessor* on behalf of the Church of Christ, his country, and his people in their oppression, would pray for them. I understood this to be a purpose for which the Lord my God had isolated me. I say *a* purpose, because this was, of course, not the only reason. Naturally, this time was also a process of purification for me. God's knife always cuts more ways than one.

The fact that I could continue to fulfil my priestly activity made me unspeakably joyful and happy. Against this National Socialistic flood which threatened to deluge everything, it was my privilege to seek the Lord's face on behalf of the people, in order that they might be strengthened in faith and that they might remain in the fear of God and persevere in the battle of faith against all manner of trials and subtle onslaughts. It was my privilege to beseech the Lord not only for the people, but also for its spiritual leaders, whose task was so weighty and whose responsibility before the Lord was so heavy. It was my privilege to beseech the Lord for all my people, that they might not be overcome by this modern heathendom, and surrender their spiritual strength. Thus I could still labour for resistance through the faith by taking my part in the prayers of the saints.

This was not without fruit, for it is our conviction that the saints have a part in the progress of the history of the Church and the world. They are laid on the golden altar before the throne of God, according to Revelation 8:3-5. Indeed:

The door is shut
The walls are dumb,
Days and nights spent in a cell.
But Christ can sanctify this hell,
To be a heaven-touched sanctum.

And thus, for my life of faith and prayer in that little oppressive cell, it was a blessed time indeed. To God be the glory.

When after three weeks of solitary confinement I was transferred to occupy a cell with others, I tried to comfort them with spiritual help. I did not preach, but I did try to reveal by my actions what quietness of faith in God is. And so I tried to help bear the burdens of others and to encourage.

With deep thankfulness I always remember the guarding and visitation personnel of the Haagsche Veer, which was at that time still sound, and proved to have a genuine love for the fatherland even at the risk of liberty and life.

Not until February 10, 1942, did I receive what might be called my sentence, from the hand of a Gestapo officer.

It ran as follows: That I as one who was a danger to the state had been taken into custody, because as intellectual head of the Reformed (*Gereformeerd*) Church of Rotterdam-Delfshaven, I had, by bringing politics on the pulpit, abused my spiritual office to stir up the Dutch people against the Great German Reich. That I would therefore be transferred to a concentration camp in Germany.

This transfer began on March 23, 1942. I was then brought to the notorious prison in Scheveningen. Thereby my detention in Rotterdam ended. With melancholy sadness I took leave of those with whom I had shared my imprisonment, but with whom I had also enjoyed such delightful fellowship, and for whom, I hope, I would still be of some help. For how many were not in need of support and comfort! Of most of those who departed before I did, I never heard anything again. Who knows what a dreadful lot they had to undergo? I think especially of my Jewish countrymen now, with whom I had such pleasant conversations in the daily fresh-air periods. Would even one of them possibly still be alive? Probably not. They likely found death by torture in the dreadful concentration camps for Jews in Germany, Poland, or Austria. Later I saw with my own eyes some of that devilishly cruel treatment of the Jews. It was nearly impossible to come through such a place alive. But I, who have been privileged to come out of the hell of a concentration camp alive by a miracle of God's care, continue to remember with deep sadness those who shared the imprisonment in Rotterdam with me.

I only stayed a short while in Scheveningen. On Saturday, April 17, 1942, I was awakened at four in the morning and commanded to be ready for immediate travel.

Where would we go? I did not know. I considered several possibilities. But my jail time was past, and I was heading for the unknown, but certainly dark, future. What would it bring? Only God knew! And in Him I trusted. He who had faithfully kept me in prison those past months, who had strengthened and encouraged me, would not leave me or forsake me now. To His holy will I had fully entrusted myself in a childlike manner, and I was at ease. Oh, indeed, I dearly hoped that all things would end in such a manner that I would be allowed to see my land and my people again, and that I would be allowed to resume that work which was so very dear to me. But, "Thy will be done!" was the basis of all my desires. If He would only remain with me, everything would be well, no matter how dark the way in which He caused me to walk. For I knew that both in life and death I am the Lord's. I belong with body and soul to Jesus. That was certain. And thus He would deal with me in the terrors of the concentration camp as He had dealt with me in the prison. *For God is good*! And Jesus keeps His promises. And He indeed gave this rich promise, "I will be with you always, even unto the end of the world." That means to be hid in Him who is Lord of lords.

Now that I look back and stand beyond all the suffering, having returned to life from death, I must acknowledge with a thankful and moved heart, "Lord Jesus, Thou didst not lie. Thou hast kept Thy Word. Thou hast been with me all the days. Never was there one moment that Thou wast not with me. Thou wast with me even when every day was no more than a day of death. Thy light was shining without any interruption in the night, which Thou in Thy great wisdom and unending goodness had prepared for me. How shall I ever be able to thank Thee for so much love, faithfulness, and strength, bestowed on me, me, who am only a very great sinner? Lord Jesus help me. Oh, help me to thankfully serve Thee, and serve Thee thankfully all the days of my life, which Thou art still willing to give me in Thy free pleasure.

"For Thou hast heard me the day I called to Thee:

> *Lead, kindly Light! Amid the encircling gloom,*
> *Lead Thou me on;*
> *The night is dark, and I am far from home,*
> *Lead Thou me on;*
> *Keep Thou my feet; I do not ask to see*
> *The distant scene; one step enough for me.*"

8. *To Dachau*

On Saturday, April 17, 1942, I was awakened at four in the morning
and commanded to be ready for immediate travel.

But to where? Would it be to the transit camp by Amersfoort,
or directly to a concentration camp in Germany? It was soon evident
that I was not to travel alone; a large transport of hundreds of
men was being prepared. It was also plain that this transport was
going directly to Germany, for we were receiving a bread ration
for a whole day. We were chased into a number of prison-vans in
double-quick time by the *Grüne Polizei* (Green Police), who brought
us to The Hague where a special train was awaiting us. The train
consisted of cars equipped with cells. In the middle of each car
was a hallway, and on both sides was a row of cells, holding four
men each.

But the train was altogether too small for our group, therefore
ten of us were locked into each cell. We had to take turns sitting
down, and we had no view outside because the windows were of
thick, dim glass. By standing on a seat, we could peek through a
little hinged window. It was thus that I had a passing glimpse of
Rotterdam. Would I ever see my city again? How far were we
going? As mentioned earlier, we had received one day's ration of
bread. But of course, they might think nothing of letting us travel
several days without food. We hoped it might be only one day.
On the way through Germany the train stopped at several prisons
and correctional institutions to drop off and pick up prisoners.
We arrived at Cologne towards dark. This proved to be the end of
the trip for a few days. We were transported in prison-vans from
the station to the prison, where, for lack of cells, we were put in
a cellar. This cellar was reasonably clean, but there were no provisions
for sleeping. Those who wanted to sleep had to settle themselves
as best they could on the floor. Some of the prisoners, who were
better at home in such situations, moved the guard to supply the
older men with a blanket. I fell into this privileged class as well.
The rest simply lay on the floor, or sat on benches and tried to
sleep with their heads on the table.

Not much came of sleeping that night. The toilet facilities consisted of a few kegs, which soon ran over, so that the air was not exactly fresh. There was no ventilation and the atmosphere became more oppressive by the hour, so we were very glad when it was time to rise.

On Sunday morning, after we had washed after a fashion and eaten, we were told to get ready. For what? Would we travel again? No, we were only to receive other quarters. Why? Was it perhaps from benevolent motives? Oh, no; this was a bomb-shelter for the guards, and it was possible that the British Air Force would bomb Cologne. It would be too bad if, in the event of a hit, a group of worthless prisoners was spared by this shelter instead of the guard personnel. So we were brought to shelter in a bathhouse. Since it had just been used, it was soaking wet, and was kept that way by a few leaking faucets. The benches were altogether insufficient for all of us, so most of us had to be content with the wet floor or the bathtubs. The blankets of the previous night had been left behind, so we were without blankets. And yet, primitive as it all was, for many of us it was a rich and blessed Sunday.

A very mixed group we were. Besides the great number of Jews and Communists and a few officers of the Dutch Army, I had discovered in our company, my old friend, Mr. H. Thijs of Amersfoort, and two pastors, Rev. Rottenburg, who had done mission work among the Jews, and Rev. M. Hinloopen, pastor of a Reformed Church (*Hersteld Verband* = Restored Federation).[24]

We soon agreed to plan a worship service. No one in our transport had any objections. I was asked to lead the service, and I eagerly seized the opportunity to comfort my fellow-prisoners with the Word of God. This was one of the most unforgettable times of my imprisonment.

An outsider cannot picture our situation to himself. We who were caught in the clutches of the Gestapo beast, torn away from home and dear ones, sat there with one another.

---

[24] These are the churches which went along with Dr. J.G. Geelkerken in 1926 after Dr. Geelkerken had been deposed from office in a Reformed (*Gereformeerd*) Church for his heretical interpretation of Genesis 3 "Did the serpent really speak?" Later these churches joined the Dutch Reformed (*Hervormd*) Church (*Nederlands Hervormde Kerk*). —Editor.

Despite the information we had received along the way from people who had been in the camps concerning the hellish conditions awaiting us, we still had no conception of what it would be like. Perhaps we were all facing certain death as martyrs. So our thoughts naturally turned towards home, and we talked together about our dear ones. Snapshots and photos appeared and made the rounds. Would we ever see them again? We thought about our beloved fatherland which was being tyrannized and plundered in such a barbaric way. Would we ever see that beloved fatherland again? Most of us were here because we had done our duty for it. Many of us were there because, in obedience to God's Word, we had resisted the principles and the measures which were a direct outgrowth of those principles, and in which we could not, according to our deepest convictions of faith, have a share. There were also those who owed their imprisonment to no other factor than that they were Jews. All were there for no other reason than that our country had been captured by a cowardly power which pinned us down. We sat there more or less deeply depressed in spirits. The separated ones!

On that Sunday morning I preached to that mixed multitude, one in its sad lot, the blessed Gospel of comfort and strength from Rom. 8:35, "Who shall separate us from the love of Christ?"

With this word I tried to comfort and encourage my fellow prisoners, and with a view to the terrors and griefs awaiting them, I tried to open to them the vision of the eternal love of Him who gave Himself for poor sinners who stretch out their pleading hands to Him.

I told them of Him who had offered Himself to the most dreadful of all suffering and death — more than any other creature could ever suffer — death on the cross and cursed by God, who had forsaken Him. Therefore, no one who clings by faith to that love of the Saviour will ever be forsaken by Him or separated from Him. Nothing and no one can separate them!

God alone knows how many received comfort and strength from this word in the grimness of the concentration camp and in the face of the martyr's death!

On Monday morning, the greatest part of our transport went further, part went to Buchenwald and another part to Sachsenhausen.

I remained behind with three Dutch Jews. Apparently, then, I was going to another concentration camp. But where to? To the same camp as my three Jewish friends? This was a painful uncertainty. Or would we presently be separated again? A few days would yield the answer.

The four of us were locked into a cell together, but only for an hour. The Bureau had discovered that I was of pure Aryan blood, to be distinguished from the Jews. Thus they were again taken out of the cell, and I remained with a Ukranian lad of fifteen or sixteen years, who had fled from a German munition factory. He was a friendly but pathetic little fellow with clear, blue eyes. A feeling of being utterly forsaken had overpowered him. He spoke no other language than his mother tongue. He was a mere child.

Later in the day our company was enlarged by a German, an Italian, a gypsy, and a Croat. The next day a sentimental Rhinelander was added. The cell was worse than filthy. The mattress and blankets were dirty. On the walls were bloody spots suggesting that lice had been smashed there. The atmosphere of the cell was that of a place infested with lice. To assure myself, I went about to investigate, and sure enough, when I lifted a mattress, I saw a family of lice which seemed to rejoice that new prey had been brought in. So I decided not to sleep on the bed but on the chairs. It was bad enough to be a prey of Gestapo lice.

The company of which I was a part is worthy of a close-up view. The German was . . . a German. He was also on his way to a concentration camp. He quarrelled repeatedly with the Italian, for that fellow told all kinds of wonderful things about the Italian dictator. Compared to Mussolini, Hitler was nothing. He did not at all conceal this from the German, but often thoroughly dressed Hitler down. The German could not swallow this. From gratitude to Adolph Hitler for sending him to the concentration camp, he defended the Führer with fiery zeal. He surely was a real German — haughty, self-righteous, convinced of the great importance of the German people before Europe and the rest of the world.

The gypsy did nothing all day but weep because he was separated from his lady-love, a fact which interested us very little.

The young Croat was a very picture of a man. He was very cultured and gave the impression of being very gifted. He spoke

German perfectly. He had no use for the German regime, and had fled from a German munition factory. I retain a very pleasant recollection of our conversations about his country and his people, which he conducted with great ardour. Alas, I lost his name and address when all my possessions were burned in Dachau. During our conversations we had to spend the time fastening snap-buttons onto cards furnished for that purpose.

Early Wednesday morning the three Jews and I were again together for further travel. Again the travelling was done in various stages. The first stop was Mainz, where we had our noon meal. In the evening we arrived at Frankfurt-on-the-Main to stay for the night. We were sheltered in a large barracks. We received no food, and there was no covering for the night. A few bales of wood-fibre were brought in, and most of us made a bed of this as best we could. It did not work well because some people thought only they were entitled to a bed, and would not let their neighbour have anything. For the first time I saw class egoism which cares only for itself and has no concern for its neighbour. How often I myself would have to battle against this selfishness as well. At the time I still had the naive imagination that this communal suffering would weave a bond of fellowship, sharing, and kindness between all who shared that suffering, but in this I was mistaken. I had to learn that communal suffering makes a man into a wolf towards his fellows. "If I have what I want, then what do I care about others" was the motto of the majority of the prisoners.

Well, this shelter was very primitive. For the few hundred men there was only one small fountain, and we all had to be finished with washing in a minimum of time. Since the journey was continued immediately, the larger part of the transport moved out unwashed.

Thus on Thursday morning we set out again. It appeared that we were on the way to Nuremberg. From this we concluded that we were going either to Dachau, or, perhaps, to a concentration camp in Austria.

Both proved to be true. The Jews were transported to the notorious murder-camp at Mauthausen in Austria, near Linz, while I was brought to the no-less notorious Dachau. Evening had come when we arrived at Nuremberg dead-tired. When we stepped off the train we were bound two by two. I was shackled to a Polish lad of about sixteen years. Being shackled was a strange sensation.

In Nuremberg we were housed in a gymnasium hall. This place was also thoroughly filthy. In the part designated for our night's lodging, we discovered to our dismay that once again there was no place to sleep. The transport which had arrived there ahead of us had taken possession of the mattresses. But the guard assured us that this was not so bad because the other transport would pull out at four in the morning, and then we could use them for a few hours. In the meantime, we had to manage as best we could. But how filthy everything was! The mattresses and covers were too foul to look at. When the other transport went out at four, I immediately crept into one of the warm nests left by the others. I fell asleep like a log after the previous five sleepless nights, but, alas, could only sleep until seven, when we were again aroused to be ready for travel. The wash bowl here also left much to be desired. It was actually used for a urinal as well as a wash basin. Repulsive as it was, I had to make use of it unless I desired to travel unwashed again. In the gymnasium hall a lively trade in lice was going on, because anyone who could prove that he had lice could receive a shower. So for a piece of bread, which was in great demand because of the hunger, one could buy a louse.

Friday morning we moved on again, this time on the last stage, as soon became evident. We travelled directly, without stopping, to Dachau, where we arrived at about five in the afternoon. Our transport, which unloaded at the Dachau station, must have contained about fifty men. There were Poles, Czechs, Luxembourgers, Germans, a man from Alsace, and I, the only Dutchman. My Jewish fellow-travellers, along with a few hundred others, stayed on the train to be shipped on to Mauthausen. Would I ever see them again? It would not surprise me if none of them ever came out of that horrible, notorious murder-camp alive. They must all have been murdered by the S.S. devils. I think especially of one of the three, named Den Hartog. He was a very cultured Jew from The Hague, and he was not far from the Kingdom of God. He took very good care of me on the trip. If they knew themselves hidden in the love of Christ for time and eternity, then even the most miserable death could not separate them from His love.

On the platform at the Dachau station, we were taken out of the hands of the *Grüne Polizei* by the S.S., who immediately prepared a very festive reception for us. They began with the raving yell,

"*Partei-mützen ab!*" (Off with those faction/party-hats.) This command was accompanied by kicking and beating whenever our response was not as fast as they desired. Then they simply knocked the lids off our heads. Thereupon we had to line up five deep and march to the buses awaiting us. As we stepped onto the buses, we expected to sit down, but soon learned that this was not the purpose of those fine gentlemen. Right behind the driver, a number of seats had been broken away, leaving a square opening. To this open square we were kicked and thrashed, so that finally we were lying stacked up in the space on top of each other, where we were to stay with our baggage all the way to the concentration camp. At the same time, we were treated to a series of curses which were wholly unfamiliar to me, but which I soon learned to understand, since they were part of the common vocabulary of the S.S. Each of us was a *Sauhund* (swine-dog) or a *Dreckpferd* (filth-horse), not to speak of worse curses.

Thus we went on our way to the camp, but even then they did not leave us alone. While we lay in a heap on top of each other thus, they treated us to a conversation among themselves, in which they unfolded their plans and methods for bringing us to our gradual martyr's-death. This was naturally not very encouraging. Finally we arrived at the camp.

Thus the long trip was finished. The end of this trip meant the beginning of a stay in this camp, notorious as "The Hell of Dachau." How long would I stay in this murder-hole? The prospects were not very encouraging. I well understood that I could expect no mercy from my persecutors. I had too much on my record for that. In fact, I had already prepared myself for an imprisonment as long as the war would last. And if, perhaps, Germany won the war — then I would probably never be free again. How much would I have to undergo? On our trip, we had already met other prisoners who told of their experiences in Dachau, which did not make us very hopeful. But the reality, as I later learned, defied all description. In this case the rumoured notoriety was far beneath the reality: Dachau was indeed a hell. Only God knew the portion of the suffering that I would receive there. Yet I knew that I was wholly in His Hand and care. Without His will no creature could move or stir against me. On Him and Him alone my firm trust was reposed. It was because of His cause that I had landed in this concentration camp, and thus my cause was wholly His. That was my comfort and peace. He would fight my case and plead my cause against an ungodly nation and deliver me from deceitful and unjust men (Ps. 43:1), whatever my lot would be and wherever my way would lead. He who had helped me hitherto and strengthened me wonderfully so that I was able to help and encourage others in their dejection, fear, and grief, would not leave me and forsake me now, but would surely help me through my suffering. And still, how dreadful that suffering would be! I knew that it would become a heavy burden of grief. But that it would be so great, so dreadful — I had not been able to imagine or anticipate. What a blessing it is that man cannot know everything in advance.

Now two things were for my mind unmoveably certain. First, that the word of the Apostle would also be fulfilled in me, which says, "For I think that God has displayed us, the apostles, last, as men condemned to death; for we have been made a spectacle (theatre) to the world, both to angels and to men" (1 Cor. 4:9). The world of angels and men look upon those who are of Christ and are reproached to see how they bear themselves in this suffering for Christ. Before the eyes of these spectators I would become a spectacle, a theatre in Dachau.

This brought with it a very weighty responsibility. Therefore I would have to suffer, not as a murderer, thief, evildoer, or as one who meddles in the affairs of other men, but as a *Christian*, as one who is the possession of Christ, and who also desires to be in his suffering willing and ready to serve Him. I would have to suffer as a member of Christ, as one who shares in the anointing of Christ, and thus also in suffering to offer my life as a sacrifice of praise, and with a free and pure conscience in this suffering, to fight against sin and the devil. Thus my spectators in this theatre in Dachau would have to see me fulfilling my three-fold office as believer.

And so it would be according to the words of Peter: "Yet if anyone suffers as a Christian, let him not be ashamed, but let Him glorify God in this matter" (1 Peter 4:16). That was my earnest prayer, that here I might also receive grace sufficient to glorify my God in this suffering.

9. In Dachau

Dachau, situated about fourteen kilometres (approximately 9 miles) northwest of München, between München and Augsburg, will go down in history as the city near which the most notorious concentration camp of the Nazi regime was located; a camp where thousands upon thousands of men of every age of life were slowly but surely tortured to death by German S.S. devils, assisted by captive German Communists. I was to spend the time from April 25, 1942, until October 9, 1943 in that camp.

When we arrived at the camp we were thrashed out of the buses in the same hard-handed way we had been put into them. Then we had to line up in front of a building outside the camp. Here we would be registered, but this did not go so quickly. Evidently the S.S. devils had not yet had enough sport with us. They picked out a few men from our group who were required to tell what wrong they had committed. Were these S.S. men interested in this? No. Their purpose was to find a few who were guilty of some moral transgression, and when they had found such a one they were really in their element. And, yes, there were a few of these in our transport. In glowing, colourful details, these men had to tell what they had committed and just how this had happened. And from the manner in which the questioners conducted the interrogation it was quite evident that these gentlemen were all too well acquainted with the field of morals. But naturally, their pretended shock and indignation knew no bounds. It was really horrible to observe this spectacle, and fortunately it was over before too many of our large crowd could be subjected to this dreadful man-baiting. Of the clergy in the group, a certain Luxembourg pastor was picked-on for this sport. He openly came out with a testimony of his faith, which brought a shower of curses on him. Later I became an intimate friend of this man. In the meantime, I myself was spared such an examination.

After all this, we were commanded to go inside the building. As many as three times we were registered here. They simply had to know everything, so that it could be recorded. We were especially asked three times for an address to which they could send notice of our eventual death.

When these duties were finished, we were made to undress, and then shaved completely bald. Then we were again dressed and photographed. In connection with this photography, another little torture-incident took place. This was as follows: I had to take my seat on a little stool unsuspecting of anything unpleasant. Innocently I sat down. Barely had I sat down when I bounced up frightened with pain. For in the seat of the stool was a little hole, and when an S.S. orderly pressed a button, a long sharp needle would thrust up through the hole, deep into the victim's seat. Terrified, he would leap to his feet again. This was the purpose of these highly cultured S.S. men. These members of this master-race found this to be such a delightful sport that they roared with glee. And you must admit that it was quite clever. Well, immediately the victim was ordered to take his seat again, and of course the same thing happened. However, this time they were robbed of their second laugh. The victim simply held himself down, needle or no needle, and that finished the pleasure of the sadists. The novelty was now worn off. With the needle deep in his seat, his picture was taken.

After this was finished, we were led into the camp itself through an iron gate. On the gate we read this promising motto: "*Arbeit Macht Frei*" (Labour Makes Free), one of those mottoes so abounding in Nazism, all of them hollow phrases, of course. Again we had to undress. It was April and still quite cold; a cutting east wind whined over the square where we stood at attention. The puddles of water were frozen from the cold, hence it was far from balmy. However, in the building where we had been photographed it had been sweltering hot, so we were soaked with sweat. And then the dreadful turn came. We not only had to undress, but they left us standing for an hour and a half in a location where all the doors and windows were purposely and deliberately thrown wide open, so that there was a dreadful draft. There we stood, shivering from the cold, and they simply let us stand. Three of the men contracted cases of pneumonia, from which they soon died. Our life of correction had begun in earnest. We had to understand this thoroughly, and for that reason we had to stand naked in that grim, icy draft.

Let me interrupt my narrative to ask and answer one question: What was really the purpose of a stay in a concentration camp? That question has only one possible answer — for *execution*, or if you will, *murder*, *annihilation*; nothing else. He who ends up in a concentration camp is, in fact, condemned to death, a death without any semblance of mercy. He is not condemned to the somewhat merciful death of the firing squad. That means one shot, and all is over. But here, one is condemned to the drawn-out, refined, thoroughly unmerciful death of living in a concentration camp. This you must bear in mind with every thing we shall further relate to you. We were bound to die. That was determined. That principle ruled everything that was done or left undone. I carried my death-sentence with me. Against this lurking death, lying in ambush for me at every turn of the road, I had to fight with all my might, every moment. At one time it well-nigh had me. Death pursued us as if we were wild game. Death was the hunter, a merciless hunter without equal. It made a horrible sport of our existence. It did not leave us alone for one moment, and its means and methods were inexhaustible. We heard death always calling, "Come, your time has arrived." Everywhere we saw this reaper standing with his merciless sickle.

It was one great dance of death, with tens of thousands prepared to partake. Every day death tried to strike us, with hunger, with murderous punishments, with exhaustion, with heavy slave-labour, with daily dread and anxiety, but it was bound to catch us; we already had this sentence in ourselves . . . (2 Cor. 1:9a). That was Dachau, the place of execution, murder, and the annihilation of thousands. And it was not kept a secret that this was the purpose of our stay. A few days after our arrival, the commander of the camp, a typical Nazi, held a welcome speech for the new-comers. The contents were as follows: "You are here through your own fault, cast out of society, and have forfeited all right to mercy in a National Socialistic community. You are worthy of death, but Adolph Hitler, in his mercy, has taken you up in this camp, so that death will not immediately take you. You might still live, but you are not to imagine that you will receive any mercy here." As long as we were not yet dead, we would be unceasingly exploited to the depth of our existence for the profit of the Third Reich, until we had been thoroughly drained of all we had. And then we would all go up through the chimney, that is, of the crematorium. There was no other end but death, the death in Dachau. There was no hope for any of us. There was only this warning: any little offense would hasten that end. And then we received a list of offenses which were worthy of death before the firing-squad. This list was so long that none of us could think of anything we could do without bringing us to our end by means of a salvo of gunfire. So much for a welcoming speech.

Well, after we had stood naked in the cold long enough, we finally received our striped prison-garb and our number. And with this, we ceased to exist. I now saw myself as a ragged beggar. The underwear was thin and ragged. It had no buttons. My top clothing was a pathetic outfit, and altogether too large.

Next we were brought to Block 13 (there were thirty in all) for newcomers, where we would have to stay for one month. Here we would get our break-in training, preparatory for camp life. We had to undergo certain courses in which we would be trained concerning the ranks of the S.S. and the laws of the camp, so that we might lead "a tranquil and quiet life in the camp." At four in the morning we arose. At noon we had one hour for dinner which was very little and very bad. In the evening between seven and eight, we had roll-call; then we had our food and went to bed.

During these courses we had all kinds of odd jobs to do. I landed in the job of window-washer. This was not heavy but very monotonous work which had to be done in our sleeping quarters, without any water. All morning I would work on one window pane, top to bottom, side to side. As companion I had a German Roman Catholic Priest who was very interested in Reformed theology, and we often had very animated religions conversations. These would immediately stop as soon as an S.S. guard approached, for conversation was strictly forbidden. This Father Kentenich helped me over my first difficulty in camp life. He was one of the few Germans with whom I could sympathize, for our German fellow-prisoners were, almost without exception, as haughty as the Nazis themselves. We kept them at a distance, also because they were not to be trusted. Besides Father Kentenich, Chaplain Rotkranz, a big-hearted and cordial Dutchman from the province of Limburg, helped me with word and deed in those first weeks. We became and have remained true friends.

After a month we were distributed into labour commandos. The commando into which I was placed was called "*Liebhof*" (Garden of Love), and was the most arduous commando of the whole camp.

My life in the camp, in which I would become a spectacle to the world and to angels and to men, had begun.

10. Dachau, the Grave of the Living Dead

When I came to Dachau, the camp counted eleven thousand prisoners. Their age varied from fifteen to eighty-four. When I was dismissed in October, 1943, the number had climbed to twenty-two thousand.

All these thousands lived a living death, for in reality we held no present existence any more. The time we spent there cannot be called history. Our whole existence there was a repetition of the previous day. Real living, participation in history, means that man lives in the rich, full, and moving present, in conscious communion with the past, so that he is open to the past and the past is open to him. At the same time, he has no living contact with the future. For that purpose he was born, thereto he was raised and educated. For that purpose he has a name, gifts, knowledge, energy, and tasks to perform. To that end he studies and prepares himself to enter into that process of life. Thus he has history and also makes it. That is human life. Life open towards the outside. The doors to the past and to the future are open to him.

But in a concentration camp a man knows nothing of this. Now that it is all past and I am writing about it, I feel how impossible it is to make it understandable to those who have not experienced these things. One must himself have gone through this terror to understand what I mean.

In the first place, the past was simply dead for us. That door was permanently closed and locked. All that was left was the memory, full of pain, a reminder that it was past for ever and never to return.

It was a locked door on which one could knock and knock, and call and clamour, but in vain. No one could ever open it. It was indeed a painful remembrance. We thought of home and wife and children and so many who were dear; we thought of work and task in life — as *in the past*; we thought of country and people and the Church, and a thousand other things to which we were bound with so many ties, as *in the past*. We well knew that it would never return. That closed past was all we had.

Thus, what was the present? It was simply a grave, a living death, worse than the dead in their graves. They at least have no memory which causes pain. Therefore the preacher praised the actual dead more than those still living.

And the same was true in regard to the future. That gate which must stand wide open to make life possible remained irrevocably closed. A man in a concentration camp has no future, no family ties — no love of wife, no children's chatter would ever sound in his ears again; he would never again help build the life of great or small; for his land, his people, and his church he would never have any meaning again. *Never! NEVER!* That thought took hold of us when we rose in the morning and ruled us when the day ended. Between those two doors — between yesterday, which was dead and gone, and tomorrow, which would never come — between those two doors we spent our existence in a camp.

That present was an endless anxious terror. What lives in the soul of a man in such a situation? It defies description. With every fibre of his existence he hungers and longs for the opening of those dreadful doors to the fullness of life. I seek words but they fail me. I still shudder from horror when I think of that existence, and even though I could heap up words of description, what man, who has never experienced such a thing, could ever understand it?

Oh, indeed, I saw how it affected the soul of men who had nothing but their hands and their teeth and their belly; whose idealism, which they had formerly held, had completely perished; they were men without faith in the living God, the faithful Father through Christ, even to men locked between those dreadful doors. I saw men become raving mad, seized by giddy, reeling bewilderment which made them into brute criminals, so that their only desire was a passion to see blood — human blood.

Do not think that only those who came from the lowest classes of society had to struggle against such mental, spiritual derailment. For each of us it was a struggle not to be overcome by this madness of such dreadful confinement. Only constant prayer made it possible to ward off the unchaining of this brute behaviour in us.

But that was not all.

We spent our lives behind barbed wire which was constantly under heavy voltage. At vantage-points, watchtowers were located from which the S.S. men held guard with machine guns in readiness, as if to say, "Beware; yesterday is dead, tomorrow is not yet; one click and your present is also gone."

Moreover, there was also the *horror of the monotonous.*

It was a society consisting of men only, nothing but men, never anything else, everywhere men; an island of men isolated from all things in the midst of the sea of the world; men who were all subject to the same lot; men without a past, present, or future, without room to live, to expand, to express themselves. There men were only bound together by one great lot, without love, without comradeship, without sympathy; full of hatred, spite, anger, and strife for every fellow man, also their fellow men in the camp. The men there always strove and battled to stretch that existence if possible, for the S.S. guards did release a few men every week, and who could know when that good fortune would befall him? And therefore, they strived to live, no matter if it cost the life of the other fellow; they stole his bread, edged him out of his working gang into a harder one, if need be; if only they, they themselves, could continue to exist. In this manner, the most perverse evils broke out, the most brute and brutal egoism, like a festering tumour.

Oh, what a world this was into which we had landed! A world of separate individuals, thrown together like corpses into a grave; living corpses who had to live in that grave but could not — the thief, the murderer, the scoundrel, the coward, the general, the politician, the priest, the preacher, the merchant, the brick-layer, the baker.

In that whole dreadful year of 1942, I never heard a laugh. The living dead do not laugh. Who laughs in his grave? We only sang those empty, hollow Nazi songs, on command. Only cursing was heard there. The most terrible blasphemies were screamed out; there was raving, bawling, fighting, and murder. A world with all the marks of hell.

Just how did that preacher in the Old Testament, that man who wrote of the vicious circle, express it? "Then I returned and considered all the oppression that is done under the sun, and behold! The tears of the oppressed, but they have no comforter; on the side of their oppressors there is power, but they have no comforter. Therefore I praised the dead who were already dead, more than the living who are still alive. Yet, better than both is he who has never existed, who has not seen the evil work that is done under the sun" (Eccl. 4:1-3).

Among thousands and thousands of living dead in their graves, I was one. I was one, who, as a child of God, had been made a spectacle to the world and to angels and to men, a theatre for the benefit of the great public that looked on to see how I would live and suffer in that grave. Would I live as a thief, a murderer, or an evildoer, or as a Christian who glorifies his God (1 Peter 4:16) by serving Him exactly, also in this awful world, as prophet, priest, and king in the office of believer? Of that theatre situation I was very deeply conscious, and I struggled with my God in prayer, that I by all means might remain faithful. And He has faithfully wrought His strength in me; He caused me to experience, by faith in His Word of promise, that in that awful present, which could not even bear the name of the present, every moment could be penetrated by the light of the presence of the grace of God in Jesus Christ my Lord. By that means I could nevertheless live, also there in that death, because His grace was sufficient for me, suffering as a Christian, not ashamed of that suffering, because it was not for murder or theft or any other crime, but solely *for the Word of God and the testimony of Jesus Christ*. And thus I could, even in the depth of my misery, glorify God, who is to be praised forever.

Blessed be God who has magnified His grace in me!

11. Dachau, the Realm of the Tortured

These living dead men were tortured every day in every conceivable manner. Whenever I think of that refined manner of torture, I ask myself, "How in God's name is it possible that people are not only capable of conceiving such tortures, but also of applying them to their fellow men?" They were often conceived by a satanic genius, by men who must indeed have sold their soul to the devil.

Our first and last torture was always and again the anxious fear of torture. With this fear we arose in the morning, in that fear we went about the entire day, and in that fear we went to bed at night. "What will happen to me next?" was the haunting question. It might come at any moment. We were prepared for it striking any moment, if not today, then, perhaps, tomorrow. But surely it would strike sometime, and yet it always struck unexpectedly.

In my case, it came all too soon — my first week in Dachau already brought my first corporal punishment. At the moment I did not know why. But this was the situation. I had been appointed with several other newcomers to carry the tea for dinner out of the kitchen. This was carried in containers or barrels holding about seventy-five litres. They were made of thick iron with a leaden lining, so they were very heavy. When they were filled they could barely be carried. Now this was one of their refined methods of torture, for after we were in the camp for a few weeks, we began to show signs of wear and exhaustion. So whenever meal-time came, the most awful spectacles might be seen. Most of the men were not equal to carrying these leaden barrels, yet *they had to*. Therefore we would see the emaciated, exhausted wretches muster all their possible strength to carry these loads. Sometimes they managed to make it. Others would break down with the load and get the boiling contents over their bodies, so that they were covered with ugly burns. But there was no mercy for the wretches. They were pounded and thrashed until they got up again. They had to carry that load, and there could be no letup. This horrible spectacle would take place several times during a meal.

But the worst was that these beatings were not administered by the S.S. men, but by the camp bosses and their cronies, who themselves were prisoners, and belonged to the German Communists. Oh, how many murders those men have on their consciences! And they did it with great delight. That was the German coming out in them. These gentlemen could not live without torturing some fellow man. Of course, they did it on orders of the S.S. men, even though it was not directly ordered. For the S.S. could not, of course, debase themselves to have any such association with Communists!

Well, I also had to help with the carrying of the tea barrels. And I happened to get a partner who was at least one-and-a-half times my size. The result was that the barrel hung at a very dangerous slant when we were carrying it. And so the boiling liquid began to stream over my hand. I let go out of pain and fright, which was a very natural reaction, of course. Immediately, an S.S. man shot forward out of the kitchen towards me and served me with a sound beating. I did not even understand why this was, and so I remained standing, dumbfounded. This caused him to increase his beating and to tell me to get to my work, even though my hand had swelled with scalding blisters — in a concentration camp no one ever has pain.

Now, why did I deserve this beating? I did not understand it at the time, because I still judged things by the rules of regular society. Later I came to understand. There was a written camp-law, and woe to the man who transgressed it. But there was also an unwritten law, and double woe to the man who broke it. And this last I had done unconsciously. The law I had broken was that of perpetual *motion*, which no one might break. That was the wearying existence of this life. It never came to rest. It knew only motion, motion, motion. Well, I had broken the law when I set down the tea barrel. For there was a row of these carriers behind me, and I had held up the progress of the movement. And therefore, I got my disciplinary beating. I then felt it as a deep humiliation, against which I stood powerless to do anything.

This was the first time I was abused. I will not relate all the instances, only a few. A few months after this affliction, I received another, for an altogether different reason.

I had a very bad case of dysentery, which was a very ordinary camp-disease. This caused me a great deal of trouble. Now I was not at work on this particular day, I do not recall why. I spent that day in Block 28, where the Polish clergy were sheltered. I had been appointed on this sweltering hot day to sprinkle the block street. The sprinkling cans were large and very heavy, and I had a violent pain in my intestines.

It was strictly forbidden to use the toilets between the hours in which the working-gangs came into the camp. Transgressions brought heavy corporal punishment. Those clean toilets had to be kept spotless with a view to possible inspection from the superiors, so that they could be convinced that the prisoners of the Third Reich were kept in very clean camps. Whether that was a tormenting regulation for those very same prisoners made no difference, of course. How I longed for the moment these working-gangs would pull in! And so I tried to control my sick system. Alas, I did not succeed. So, rather than risk soiling my clothes, I risked going to a toilet. Nothing ventured, nothing gained.

I lost, because the boss of Room 4 in my block, a German Communist, had been lying in wait for me. Barely had I reached the toilets when he stormed in on me and began to beat me in my face with his belt, until the blood dripped down. But this still did not satisfy him. He wound himself up to a wild rage and kicked me in my side, out the door, and up the street, so that I had no time to adjust my clothes.

Naturally, we all tried as much as possible to avoid these torturous disciplines, so the watchword became, "Beware that you do not strike the eye, that you do not draw any attention."

One of the most dreaded tortures of Dachau was receiving twenty-five, fifty, or one hundred strokes with a rod. This object was really not an ordinary stick or club. It had the name *Ocksenschwanz* (ox-tail). For the smallest offense we were sometimes condemned to this punishment, for example, if we had "organized" a few potatoes, or if we had stolen a handful of potato peelings from the garbage can because we were hungry. Then the whole camp would have to be eyewitnesses of this execution, often late in the evening after roll-call. This execution was carried out with a specially made wooden horse. It is said that the S.S. men of

Buchenwald had given assignment to a prisoner to invent an instrument that could be used for corporal punishment. That prisoner invented this horse. And the story goes that the first one on whom this new torture apparatus was tried out was the inventor himself. This horse can best be compared to a narrow table. The condemned person was laid upon it on his belly. His hands were tied down to the forelegs of the horse, and his legs to the hind legs of the horse. Next a strap was tied around his middle so that he could not move. Then his clothes were stripped down and on either side an S.S. executioner took his position armed with an ox-tail. While they counted the strokes, they would strike exactly on the tip of the spine, causing an inhuman agony. Often they would deliberately smash the kidneys with their blows. When a tortured man died of this treatment, they reported to the family that he had died of kidney trouble. Often when one was condemned to fifty blows, he would receive only twenty-five. Was this a mercy? Not at all. He would get the other twenty-five later, and in the meantime he was warned not to go to a doctor to have his lacerations treated. That would certainly be in order, for the twenty-five strokes made his buttocks into a jelly-like bloody mass. And so the poor creature would doctor it as best he could when he found opportunity. But the end of the story was that the whole mass began to fester terribly. And when it was well festering, he would get the balance of those fifty strokes.

There you have proof of highly cultured German Nazism. Let us never forget that our own countrymen who were members of the N.S.B. and who made common cause with these Germans are and remain responsible for these tortures.

Another torture was to be shot while *attempting* to escape. In my labour commando this happened once. We were all required to wear caps in camp, for whenever we met an S.S. man, we had to show our respect by removing them. Now it happened that one morning, the S.S. guards were in a very sportive and jocular mood. This always filled us with great anxiety, for we knew that at any moment something dreadful could happen. Something dreadful did happen. One of the S.S. guards grabbed a cap from a young Pole and threw it a distance away. What was the fellow to do? Two possibilities were open: either to run and get his cap and put it on, or to leave his cap and continue his work bareheaded. Either choice would be very dangerous. He chose the first, raced for his cap, and the S.S. man simply drew sights on him and shot him right there for "attempting to escape."

The dread of torture took hold on all of us because it was, "*him* today; perhaps *me* tomorrow."

I will never forget Pentecost Sunday of the year of our Lord 1942. On that day the Church of Jesus Christ assembled to proclaim the Gospel of Pentecost, and to bring to remembrance that blessed outpouring of the Spirit who brings eternal joy into the sad hearts of men.

On that day the whole camp received punishment. Nobody knew why. Most likely because of the passion of the S.S. to thoroughly ruin the Sunday of rest. What was the punishment? After morning roll-call, we were commanded to take everything out of our sleeping quarters into the street. The mattresses had to be piled five high. Next the sheets, blankets, and pillows. Then we had to dismantle all the bedsteads and carry them out. Suddenly we all had to step forward and stand at attention. It was now seven in the morning. How long must we stand?

Hour after hour wore on. Noon hour passed — no dinner. We stood at attention, for the S.S. men were lying in wait for us. Some fell; here one caved in, there another collapsed. They were kicked to erect positions again. "When the command is '*Stand*,' that means '*Stand*,' does it not!" We remained standing, hour after hour. We could not keep ourselves erect any longer, but we *had to. Stand, stand, stand.* The whole long day.

At noon, a terrible thunder storm broke out over Dachau. The rain poured down. We stood. Our clothes were soaked; the water streamed out of our sleeves and pant-legs. We stood. Our bedding, mattresses, blankets, sheets, and pillows, became soaked. We stood, until finally, at seven in the evening, we received the command to disband. Then we had to drag our bedsteads back inside and assemble them, bring in our wet mattresses and bedding, make our beds, and finally, dead tired, we could sleep and take our rest.

Rest? Don't ever think so! There was another torture awaiting us. In a concentration camp nobody must rest, you know, because tiredness does not exist there. So they violated our night of rest also.

How glad we were when we finally lay on our bunks after such a day. Glorious sleep at last! Rest; no more thinking; we could be deeply sunk away, knowing nothing of that naked reality which was our lot for a few hours. We had a rhyme which said,

What is best in the K.Z.?[25]
The bread-time and the bed.

But neither bread nor bed were safe from these sadistic bloodhounds. We slept, but were sleeping only an hour before they commanded, "All out of bed!" And when we were up and wide awake, we could go back to sleep. This awakening was merely to ruin our night's sleep and its resting effect. This was not done once a night. Oh, no, sometimes even five times. And all this hurried our existence along to the point of annihilation.

Besides this, there was also the torture of penal-exercising, which came when, dead-tired, we were ready for bed after evening roll-call. Then they would have our section do exercises for a few hours. We had to stand up, fall down flat, and rise on our haunches, all to the accompaniment of kicks and blows. Or they would ruin our Sundays with this burden, for without torture and dread of torture, life in the camp was not complete.

We were also hounded with "magic bed-making," at four in the morning. First we had to insert a stick through the centre slit of the mattress, to fill out the corners until they were beautifully square. And quick, hurry! Then we laid one blanket, folded, on the straw-mattress, in such a way that a short border covered the edge. And quick, hurry! Then we had to stretch the sheet over the mattress and blanket, as smooth as a board. And, finally, the second blanket folded over the pillow so that it looked like a waterfall. And quick, hurry! And this all had to be smoothed with an "ironing board," without a wrinkle. "Beware that your waterfall pattern is in an exact line with all the other waterfall beds the whole length of the ward —" for the S.S. man is a worshipper of the straight line, just like all Germans. "Woe to you if your waterfall pattern is a fraction of an inch out of line with the others, for then you

---

[25] K.Z. = *Kon-Zentration* (*Lager*) = Concentration (camp).

will spend your noon-hour without food, making beds, and not only once, but at least ten times. Or you will be caned." Thus they kept us in suspense of possible tortures.

Our lockers were also a means of torture. They had to be kept whiter than snow by using sand-paper. And so they would make us scour and scour all day Sunday. Our aluminum mess-dishes were to be polished until they shone. That would cost us our Sunday afternoon. Our handkerchiefs and dish-cloths had to be folded and hung in our lockers according to a very definite regulation. Our dishes, plates, and drinking-cups had to be placed just so, only so many fractions of an inch from the edge. And, "Woe to you if it was not exactly according to prescription." Everything was designed to cause us torture.

Sometimes they reckoned that a prohibition against sitting at meals was an especially good means of torture. Hence, we sometimes had to stand at meals for a month. Or in an exceptional case, we might have to sit on our knees at the table. And, as for the clergy, they took special delight in afflicting them for a month at a time by withholding their meagre portion of bread from them.

Resting during the day between work periods was forbidden. After we had eaten our meal at noon, which always had to happen in as little time as possible, we were chased out of our rooms into the street, rain or shine. And there we had to walk back and forth or simply stand. Then we would want to lean against the wall for just a moment because we were so tired. But we had to beware, for if we were caught in the act, which happened often, for they were constantly spying around, then we would get a beating. "Move, move, always keep moving." Sit on the curb a moment? We didn't dare, because it was punished with a kick in the ribs. "Walk or stand, do not sit. Never sit down. Nowhere. Move. Keep moving."

The leadership of the camp was always on the look-out for new means of torture. They were very inventive. My first ward-boss — he was a good fellow — told me once of a special torture the S.S. devils had contrived for him. He had been arrested immediately upon the seizure of power by Hitler, that mass-murderer. He was No. 9. After he had spent six years in this camp, he was told on a certain morning that he was dismissed. He did not understand it at all. But it proved to be true. The S.S. took him to the train and he got on board. The train pulled away, and he was free. At the third train-station, the S.S. came aboard and got him out of the coach. It had been a *mistake*. He had to return to Dachau. Now, of course, that was no *mistake*. It was simply a means of torture. They had deliberately made him glad with a soap-bubble.

In July 1942, we had a week of rain. We had worked the entire week in *Liebhof*, and we were soaked through. Our clothes would not dry anymore. At last it was so muddy that we could no longer accomplish anything in the field anymore. The leaders saw that we would only spoil things, so they decided to keep us in, since it was still raining on the sixth day. Well, would that mean a day of rest? Whoever thought so was off track. In a concentration camp a day of rest is not known. So what did they do with us? We were four or five thousand men strong, and we had the "liberty" to go into an empty room. *And there we had to stay standing.* This room was not built for such a great number. So we stood with our dripping clothes crowded against each other. From six until eleven o'clock we had to stay standing. No one was equal to that. One after another began to sag down to the ground. At last we all sat packed on top of each other. And that was the moment of feasting for the torture-devils. They had known that we were not equal to that long period of standing, and that we would finally be sitting, contrary to orders. That is what the gentlemen were waiting for. When they had figured that by this time things had developed far enough, they suddenly threw open the doors, and armed with sticks and accompanied with loud yells, they leaped in among the mass of men and began to beat us on our heads as hard as they could. Everybody tried to scramble to his feet. But that worked poorly, since we fell on one another. Men were trampled under foot. I landed on a Polish priest who was dying. The poor fellow! We fought with one another to get to our feet. Finally, all were pretty well erect again, and then the sadists left us alone. But it was a period of hellish terror that we lived through there.

The next morning it was still raining. But we went out to the job. We had to work for a while, but we could not, since the rain continued to stream. We stood out in the middle of the field, bent, with our backs to the wind like cows in a pasture, while the merciless rain splashed down on our dripping clothes. We were glad to hear the bell ring. Would we go back to camp? We shivered from the cold. But no, we were only allowed to shelter under a shed. And there we crowded constantly closer against each other to gain a little warmth from one another. We were a tangle of dripping skeletons wearing zebra stripes. Those against the wall were almost pressed to death and those in front shivered from the cold. Then, after we had stood thus like a troop of miserable pariahs for an hour, the rain eased up a little and we had to go to work again. The commander and the boss had planned some work in that hour. However wet and cold we were, we got the job of lugging a great number of logs from one side of the property to the other. We first had to heave them on our shoulders and carry them. We could not, and so a number of us collapsed in this attempt, but we *had to*. And when we had finished, we got mattocks and spades and had to dig up and loosen a piece of earth, and remove the many stones from it. For many of us this day was really the last day.

All of these tortures were, however, subservient to the one main purpose of our stay in the camp, namely, to bring about our death penalty, our execution over a long period of time. By gradual but sure exhaustion, we were hounded to death. For the chimney of the big incinerator was waiting for us — for each and every one of us. Indeed, the death which Adolph Hitler and his murderous gang had planned for us, and which he brought about by torture, was no pleasant death. *It was nothing less than the disposal of a mess of vermin.* It was merely letting one sink down like an old piece of worthless rag into the stinking pool of the decay and disruption of life and living.

Whoever has looked this death in the face, such a debasing death, must surely laugh aloud at sentimental, genteel, and ladylike warbling with crocodile tears that one must not weep about the sweet experience of death. A sweet experience? Death is never sweet. But this dying, by one of a thousand most humiliating and debasing means of torture, causes one to cry out, "Oh, my God! How awfully abominable is this dying." And one would accuse before God and men all those who are responsible for such dying of their fellow-men, and who *desired*, *planned*, and *willed* this kind of death.

Ah, I was exhausted by all those afflictions. I have had days that, in its most literal meaning, I *dragged* myself forward. My feet were sore with blisters and festering. My shoes were much too small. I couldn't get bigger ones, because they simply did not want to give them to me. Every morning I had to twist my sore feet into those small shoes. That was torment. And if only I could keep them on the whole day, I would get used to it. But no, we often had to take them off. And then the torment would be repeated.

My body was wasted away. I literally became skin and bones. My head had become a skull from which the skin had been forgotten to be removed. My calves had become skin without flesh. My ribs pressed through my skin. I could hardly sit down because it hurt so much. I only weighed ninety pounds, for I had lost nearly seventy pounds, so when I got up at 4:00 A.M., I was already very exhausted. In our room the ward-boss already stood with a rod, ready to strike us if our beds were not made up according to the regulations. Even if he only looked at me, I would cringe, because I knew from experience that he would manage to strike me in a very cruel manner.

Then we had to deal with the insane pace of life at the block. This was not humane. It was nothing else but insane. Even worse: It was the destructive pace of Hell!

"Wash yourself! Hurry!" Oh, the misery of so many men in such a small washroom that everyone bumped into each other and many cursed each other. "Hurry, eat your meal!" The whip of the slave driver struck, but I *couldn't* go on any longer. I was exhausted, but had to dress. "Dress yourself! Hurry!" I hurriedly dressed myself as one also insane. I couldn't do it, but I had to. I had to keep up with the insane pace of the camp. Otherwise I would be defeated in my battle, and that was the last thing I wanted. Then I had to get ready for the morning roll call. Finally a moment of rest! While we marched towards the place of the roll call, my heart sang one Psalm after another. A Psalm of praise was succeeded by a Psalm of lamentation. I needed both, and my heart could sing both in the night of my tormented life.

While we stood and rested at the place of the roll call, I had the opportunity to send up my morning prayer to ask my faithful Father for strength and His comforting presence, to suffer as a Christian, able to glorify his Father in these conditions, and able to look the world of men and angels square in the face. And then I knew it again: This spectacle in Dachau was for me a joyful day, a feast-day in communion with my God. And that was all I needed. Presently we would march away again. But I could now go on. My tiredness seemed to fade away just a little, and at least I did not feel as exhausted, though I still really was. God, my God, was making true to me the word which He once spoke through His servant Isaiah: "He gives power to the faint, and to those without might He gives strength." Presently at work in *Liebhof*, the hounding would begin again, but it would not affect me or harm me. I would not hear the harsh refrain of the boss: "Hurry, hurry, hup, hup, hup!" anymore. The Lord was with me, and He is good. I was so rich and blessed with Him. I could not go on any longer, but I wanted to, for I was determined to *live*. I wanted to live to serve Him again in The Netherlands, by proclaiming the holy Gospel and testifying in the congregation of Jesus Christ, that we have a God who never, never lies, but always fulfils and keeps His word.

Thus my way was made through these tortures, looking to Jesus, the Author and Finisher of our faith, who for the glory that was set before Him, endured the cross and despised the shame. Oh, my God, I thank Thee, that I was always enabled in my tortures to keep looking by faith to Jesus, and that there was not a moment that I did not see Him. I thank Thee that this hymn was always with me:

I know in whom my hope is founded
Through ever-changing day and night.
Thou hast me with Thy love surrounded;
Thou art my Rock, I trust Thy might.
When once life's evening veils enshroud me,
I'll bring, though worn by ills and strife,
For every day Thou hast in Dachau *allowed me*
Thee higher praise, O God of life!

Indeed, no one who waits on Thee will be put to shame (Ps. 25:3). Thus I, who had become a theatre in Dachau to the world, to angels, and to men, was seen by my spectators. And thus my God has also seen me. I know that it was not by my strength, but solely by His power, and for the glory of His eternal good pleasure.

12. Dachau, the City of Slaves

The third Reich was similar to the ancient Roman Empire in that it created a separate slave-caste. Thus this creation of Adolph Hitler was not strictly new. Of course, we know that Nazism was badly afflicted with the imitating germ. The slaves of this imitation-dictator were utterly without any rights. These slaves were those who had undertaken something against the National Socialist State or Party. Even the smallest offense was punishable, and the punishment those offenders were subjected to was that they had no place any more in the National Socialist social structure. They were cast out as unworthy and worthless, and just as vermin is exterminated, so they were to be exterminated, not suddenly, but gradually, with a tantalizing, refined, protracted extermination. During the time that elapsed between their expulsion and their final death, they were squeezed for the benefit of the Third Reich like one squeezes a lemon dry of its juice. And when the last drop of value was squeezed out, they were cast away like a dried peel. Those were the slaves of Adolph Hitler, men, women, and children of every rank and position.

A slave has no name. He is a nameless thing. He has a number. Or rather, he *is* a number. Among the thousands of slaves at Dachau, I was No. 29807.

My first ward-boss was No. 9. Who can fathom the ocean depths of grief and misery that lay between those two numbers? But it was still worse that this creature who was degraded to a number was constantly reminded of the fact that there was a time when he was not a number, but a human person, with a name, a date of birth, and a place of birth, a real, living, ordinary human being, like all others in human civilization. The means by which the painful consciousness of that fact was kept fresh in his mind, was the special formula for reporting oneself. When one had to appear somewhere, for example, for examination or interrogation, then he had to use that formula. He would have to take off his cap, stand at rigid attention, heels meeting, and say, "Prisoner Knoop, Herman; born December 3, 1891, in Amsterdam." That *was*; that was in the past, the irrevocable past. Therefore he would continue, "No. 29807 obediently reports." That was his present state, until death.

That we were slaves also meant that we had to be *marked*. On our clothing, on our coats and pant legs, we had, besides our number, also a coloured triangle. From the colour could be read what our crime against the National Socialist State or Party had been. Our *sins* were *marked* on us. The political prisoners had a red triangle, the anti-social prisoners had a black triangle, the homosexuals were decorated with a pink one, the criminal evil-doers, who were considered unfit to ever return to a place in society, were marked with a green one, and the Jehovah's Witnesses or Bible distorters were marked with a purple triangle.

The fact that a man's sin was marked on him gave occasion for repeated harassments. He would be walking on the camp-street or working, when suddenly some S.S. official would become very concerned about his case. Then hell was let loose. He would be questioned, and have to make confession of the crime of which he had made himself guilty. And then he would be pestered and tantalized in the hope that he would make some slip of word or temper that would not please the gentlemen, and they would make him feel thoroughly, in a very painful manner sometimes, that he was nothing but a despicable slave. A prisoner is nothing but filth.

There were two groups of prisoners who got the large share of this misery. They were the homosexuals and the clergy. The first, naturally, so that these virtuous S.S. men could delight themselves with all manner of unsavoury things. And the second group gave them opportunity to belch their hatred and contempt against God and His Christ. Several times, after I had obediently confessed why I was imprisoned, I had to hear such a flood of blasphemy. The most terrible part of it was that you had no defence whatever. For — you were a *slave*.

You were also a slave in that you did not have *your own clothing*. Of course not. Was not your garment a sign of your personality? And a slave had no personality. He was a thing, an object, with which they did as they pleased. Therefore, immediately upon entering the camp, we were stripped of our clothing. Every physical abuse I felt as humiliation, but the deepest humiliation of all was that I had to remove my clothing and have it taken away from me. The worst of this was, no doubt, the emphasis of transition from human being to slave; they created a kind of vacuum by letting me stand naked for about an hour and a half while waiting for my slave garb. And what a garb! Monotonous uniformity of striped blue-and-white which everyone wore. Numbers, slave numbers, which could not be distinguished from one another, and for which variation of dress had ceased to exist. It was the humiliation of levelling equalization. For — one was a *slave*.

And one was a slave in that he had to do the work of a slave. If one said that he had gifts, culture, knowledge, or was a specialist in some field, he would hear the retort, "Man, what are you saying?" There, no one had gifts or culture or knowledge. There, everyone had simply *nothing*. If one said he was an engineer, a doctor, a statesman, a pastor, a priest, a general, or a craftsman, he would be answered, "Man, you are mistaken." There, nobody was an engineer, doctor, pastor, or anything you could name. There, no one was anything. If he said he was an intellectual, he would be asked, "Man, where did you get that idea? No one is an intellectual here. Here everyone is a nothing, for you are all slaves. That is what you are here, and that is what you do here. A slave does slave labour!"

In my second week in Dachau — remember, I had no gifts or knowledge, I was not a pastor, I had nothing, I was a slave — I had to be busy sorting rags. With my bare hands I had to untangle the filthy, greasy rags, and pile them up nicely and neatly from early morning till supper time. It was utterly aimless work, for in the evening they mixed the whole pile through each other again, and in the morning I could begin all over again. Ah, no, one was nothing, had nothing, could do nothing. For — one was a *slave*.

A few weeks later I was put to work on an immense manure-pile. My feet were all broken open and festering. The filthy manure-dregs oozed in my shoes and sucked at the wounds on my bare feet. My hands were also broken and festering. And now the shameful part of it was not that I had to work on a manure pile, but this work had no other purpose than to make me feel that I was only a slave. For with my broken, festering hands, I had to find every minute piece of glass and make a little pile of it. It was, of course, utterly useless work, this dressing of the manure-pile. But one was a *slave*.

As a slave, one also had the lot of a slave, of course. And that meant, above all, that he had to be obedient; as obedient as a cadaver. Above all, do not think: A slave must not think. I was in my block for only a short time when I made the unguarded mistake of saying to a "superior," "I think . . ." "What!" he answered. "You still think?" And he gave me a blow in my face. One was never to have any feelings, and if he did, never let it show. Obedience and nothing else is the lot of a slave. And for the rest, "Keep your mouth shut;" that was all.

Everything that was interpreted as disobedience cost one an extra punishment. For example, working in a discipline commando four Sundays from sunrise to sunset without food. That meant pulling a huge, heavy roller back and forth the whole day. He was a first-class slave. There they were, a troop of emaciated skeletons, exhausted, toiling in the burning sun or the drenching rain. That was the slave's lot.

That one was a slave also meant that he had no right to food. Of course not. A slave was to be done away with. Just how he was eliminated made little difference. One of the means was to remove him by starvation. Therefore our portion of food was so carefully planned, that a gradual but sure death by starvation was inevitable. I myself barely escaped this death by starvation. And how many of my friends have I not seen succumb. That was part of the execution. After I had been in Dachau a month, I was assigned to a commando with the beautiful name of *Liebhof* (Garden of Love), but which in our camp jargon was called *Friedhof* (Cemetery), because of all the men who died in that outfit. In slack times it numbered one hundred men, and in busy times it was expanded to about two hundred. It was one of the most arduous and awful of all the commandos. The pace of labour was accelerated every day. The commander was a genuine Nazi beast. So also was the commissary. They ground us like coolies and serfs, and knew no mercy for the sick and weak.

The bosses, who were afraid to lose their jobs, and who, like all servile Germans, always crawled for their superiors, helped along with this abuse; even though they themselves were prisoners, they pushed other prisoners like hounded game. They demanded of us more than our one hundred percent. And because this was the most arduous commando, the clergy, especially, were assigned to *Liebhof*. This was the easiest way to dispose of these parasites. All of the *Liebhof* slaves were hungry, emaciated, and exhausted creatures. They were a miserable troop as they marched along, singing, to the place that became the place of death for many of them. The heavy labour and insufficient food made many of them victims to starvation. Sometimes they would simply fall dead beside me. At first this was frightening, but at last I became accustomed to it. This starvation-death was accompanied by dysentery, and those whom starvation passed by, fell victim to this disease. I have seen twenty-three out of one hundred men fall dead from dysentery and hunger on *Liebhof* in one day. Of course, this was an exceptional day, but no day passed without some men dying of their slave-lot.

When I had been on the *Liebhof* commando for two months, I was, along with two others, already a senior member. Those before me had already died, or were awaiting their death in the hospital.

The worst of it was that we had to carry our dying comrades back to camp on our shoulders. That was a lugubrious procession. Imagine a troop of wrecks, who could hardly drag themselves along, carrying the dead and dying on their shoulders. Often the carrier collapsed and the dead burden would roll over the road. It was a repulsive sight. And, as if all this was not bad enough yet, we were required to sing as we went. On the barren road from *Liebhof* to Dachau, the death-procession would sing:

> *Man lives but once,*
> *And then no more.*

We clergy changed this to:

> *Man lives here once,*
> *And then even more.*

Yes, the lot of the slave in Dachau was complete.

At the end of July, 1942, it seemed that this slave's lot of starvation would also bring my end. Starved and dead-tired, I looked like a ghost from the realm of the dead who had gone astray to earth. How long would I still live? I was wholly unequal to the heavy field work and caved in repeatedly. When I marched to work, two comrades bore me up until we reached *Liebhof*. Yet I never lost the conviction that I would survive it all. By superhuman exertion I kept going until August 26, 1942; then I collapsed and had to be brought to the hospital.

Physically I was done for, but spiritually I was stronger than ever. When they brought me to the hospital and I was losing consciousness, I heard the orderly say, "Just let him be; in a couple of hours he'll be dead anyway." But I said to myself, "No, not dead in a couple of hours."

> *I shall not die, but live, and praise Him;*
> *In song His deeds my theme shall be.*
> *Although the LORD has sorely chastened,*
> *He has from death delivered me.*[26]

This slave's lot would not be mine. They, indeed, said, "He is a slave of Hitler and must die." But my God said, "He is a slave of Jesus Christ, a child of the King; he shall not die, but he shall live." My trust was established in Him in that hour of my deepest misery. That was revealed by the spectacle I was to the spectators: the world, angels, and men. In myself I had the sentence of death, in order that I would not trust in myself, but in God, who raises the dead.

---

[26] Psalm 118:4b (*Book of Praise*).

13. Dachau, a Den of Murder

When one entered the Dachau Concentration Camp through the iron gate, there was a motto which held a promise. That promise was, "Labour Makes Free." Thus, to become free from the bondage of this murder-camp, one had to work. Of course, this motto was like all National Socialist mottoes — a lie, although labour brought freedom to every coolie who toiled until he fell dead.

Upon entering the gate, one came to the place where all the men had to report twice a day to be counted. At the right of this entrance stood a large complex of buildings containing kitchen, washrooms, laundry rooms, cobblery, clothing-warehouse, etc. These buildings were constructed by the prisoners who were seized at the time of Hitler's grasp for power. My first ward-boss, No. 9, told me a dreadful story about this labour. He had seen it with his own eyes and I can easily believe it. One day when we were discussing the horrors of the camp this boss said to me, "Did you know that there are people built into those walls?" I thought he meant that they had cemented corpses into the walls. But that was not what he meant. He said that it often happened that the S.S. men would have their sportive days. And this sportiveness boded very little good for us. Well, on one such day, when these gentlemen were in a very jolly mood, one of them seized the first prisoner at hand who was toiling at the pouring of cement, lifted him up, and tossed him alive into the cement-mixer. And thus this unfortunate creature was mixed into the cement and built into the construction.

What was that motto again? Was it not "Labour Makes Free?" Was that not true? It was murder!

This terrible story is a bloody illustration of the fact that Dachau was a den of murder on a large scale. They murdered deliberately. That is, the sentence of death was simply carried out in some such manner.

Just another illustration. When I came to the camp on April 25, I soon learned that just a few days before, a well-known pastor of the Dutch Reformed (*Hervormd*) Church of Rotterdam had been murdered. It was Rev. Rutgers. He had been housed in the block where the Polish clergy were kept. The block-boss and the ward-boss were a couple of thoroughly seasoned sadists. Both were Germans, and, naturally, prisoners as well as the rest. For some reason or other they made an attack on Rev. Rutgers, beat him and kicked him from one end of the room to the other, and worked themselves into a frenzy when they saw blood. Bleeding and grievously wounded, he had to be moved to the hospital, where he shortly afterwards died of his wounds. That was how the death sentence implied in his imprisonment came to be carried out in this den of murder.

Now there were *special places* in the camp that were really designed *for such murders*. We were dreadfully afraid of these places, and did everything we could to avoid them.

One of the places that filled us with dread was the *hospital*. That was a modern murder-den *par excellence*. Anyone who went to the hospital was always tortured with the idea: "Will I perhaps be murdered here?" Its motto could have been: "He who enters here, dismiss all hope." "Why?" you will ask. Because they practised vivisection here, not on animals, but on living people. Prisoners became guinea-pigs. They were the objects of "scientific" experimentation. They experimented with various serums against diseases on them.

There was, for example, a malaria clinic. By means of malaria mosquitoes, they first developed the infection in prisoners, preferably in clergyman, and then "treated" them for malaria. The results were most horrible. Many died of the experimentation. They were simply murdered. Others held on to life, but were, of course, murdered for the rest of their existence. They became unfortunate wretches who were constantly overcome by resurgent attacks of malaria, so that they had to undergo that helpful "treatment" again and again.

Terror filled us when we had to report in line and the "malaria professor" would come and pick his experiment-victims out of our slave-gang.

There was also an edema clinic (for those with legs broken open from starvation-inflamation), where they "experimented" with "cures" for starvation-inflamation. I shall never forget that day in November 1942, when we had to report in person because the edema clinic needed more guinea-pigs. My ward-boss, who was very well disposed towards me, said, "Don't you go, but hide up in the attic-room until I call you." Among those reporting was my friend, Rev. Jan Willem Tunderman, pastor of the Reformed (*Gereformeerd*) Church in Helpman, Groningen. Alas, he was chosen because he had open legs. Before he was taken to the hospital, I still had a talk with him. It was the last time I saw him. He was very much under the impression that he would not come out alive. I tried to comfort and encourage him by pointing to the power of God who would surely deliver him if that was His purpose. But, I told him, however the way might lead, he must give himself wholly up to the Lord's will. I was allowed to see him go comforted. Yet it was not that he doubted the power of God. Nor did he have a conflict to submit himself to the will of the Lord. There was something else that troubled him. It was the same thing that I sensed in so many who lived by faith. It was that conviction of being devoted to death. This he could not shake off. Just as I never lost the conviction that I would some day come out of that camp alive, so he had the firm conviction, sometimes stronger than at other times, that he would have to die in the concentration camp.

Before this strong conviction on his part my words of comfort had to give way. So I comforted him with the fact that Christ never leaves His own, but is with them all their days, and that this is the most important of all, that *He* remains.

So he departed, that man with whom I had so many glorious conversations, with whom I also made plans for the future if we were released. He was still planning to write a book. Thus he went to meet his death, and I never saw him again. For six weeks they experimented with him, and on the 26th of December, 1942, he passed away as a result of this. Murdered! On that day his soul joined the throng of the martyrs' souls under the altar, and he has joined the church which wars by means of the prayer, "How long, O Lord, holy and true, wilt Thou not judge and avenge our blood on those who dwell on the earth?" God heard and answered this prayer.

While I am writing this, a sermon on 2 Cor. 4:11-15, dealing with, "The Sacrifice of Life in the Service of Resurrected Life" lies before me. Rev. Tunderman preached this sermon on April 27, 1941. It was as if he was sketching his own life and that he already felt what was to befall him. His life and death stood under the pressure of this theme. He was a spectacle to the world and to angels and to men, that he might give his life as a willing offering in the service of the resurrection of life. *Service* was its theme. That is the way his great Observer, Jesus Christ, his Lord, also viewed this life. He is the One who led this servant to offer his life. And in this the great Servant showed His own life. He caused him to yield his life; in the future He will cause it to produce its fruit.

When she heard of his death, Rev. Tunderman's wife, who died shortly later, wrote, "I have believed, therefore I have spoken." This was the motto of them both, who now sing this Psalm where faith has become sight.

Besides these experimentations there were others. There was also a typhoid clinic, and one for kidney stones and gallstones.

There was still another quarter made to serve for murdering. It was the so-called Invalid Block. Here were quartered all the coolies who, because of old age, weakness, or other physical defects, were no longer able to continue their work, but who could not be taken into the hospital, and were still not polite enough to die and be out of the way. So these murderers would just give these impolite ones a little hand in becoming removed. Leave it to them. For a slave who cannot work and still does not die cannot be tolerated. And so at stated times a transport of these was made up out of the Invalid Block. These people were then taken to the "convalescent-home," as they called it.

Whenever we saw such a transport of wrecks leaving again, we could not restrain our tears. It was a pitiable sight to see them totter away with their little bundle of possessions under their arm. Were they really going for convalescence? We knew better. They were going to the gas-chamber to be disposed of like rats. Therefore they were nick-named "Ascension Commandos." They were simply murdered by this highly-civilized German culture.

My friend Dr. Kornelis Sietsma, pastor of the Reformed (*Gereformeerd*) Church in Amsterdam-South, was also quartered in the Invalid Block. Was this because he was an invalid? Actually not, he had had the misfortune of having boiling tea spill over his hand, just as I had. These scald-wounds would not heal, as was characteristic of all wounds there because of the bad diet. But the same boss who was responsible for the death of Rev. Rutgers was also responsible for bringing Dr. Sietsma to the Invalid Block. This beast, said to be an S.S. man under discipline, hated God and the clergy. If he could deal one of the clergy a deadly blow he would not fail. So, when Dr. Sietsma could not work because of his injured hand, it was this gentleman who had such pleasure in dealing a blow at this servant of the Lord, that he eagerly grasped the chance to assign him to the Invalid Block. Such a disposal was planned for Kees, but the Lord had different plans and did not leave him in the hand of the enemy. Shortly before a load was made up to be disposed of, he was struck by a severe case of dysentery, which soon ended his life. I also lay in the hospital at the same time.

By Kees Sietsma's death, a gifted and courageous man passed away. How full of courage he always was! How fully he lived out of faith so that he was a support to many! How thankful I am that I was able to associate with him in the barren existence of Dachau! Until the hour of his death he remained a faithful witness of Jesus Christ. One day also the harvest of his life will become manifest, for he was always steadfast and unmovable, always abounding in the work of the Lord. And this labour in the Lord was not in vain. It was the labour which he willingly released when his Master said, "Come!" He was ready. He himself once characterized it as a readiness which does not exclude the labour here on earth, but actually encourages and stimulates it, because all labour advances the Kingdom when it is done in reverent fear. He was also ready any moment to stop when the trumpet proclaimed, "The King is coming. Assemble from all the ends of the earth!" Thus Kees Sietsma laid aside all the work he had in hand when his King called, "Come, enter into the joy of your Lord!"

With melancholy sadness I also think of my friend Rev. Johannes Kapteyn, pastor of the Reformed (*Gereformeerd*) Church in Groningen. He also died in Dachau, or rather, was murdered there. When I think of Jo Kapteyn, I see this tall young man before me, and my emotions surge up when I realize that I shall henceforth have to miss his faithful, beautiful friendship in my life. We were so fully one in heart. We both had the same view of the life of our Reformed (*Gereformeerd*) Churches. We both had the same expectation as to what would happen in our churches in the future.[27] We also had the same conception of our necessary ecclesiastical resistance, and were greatly disappointed about the gross negligence in this respect.

Heavy was the path which Jo had to travel, and great was his suffering, but his faith flourished beautifully. The Lord did great things for him. He carried his sufferings, which were much heavier than any of ours because he was very concerned about his family, from whom he did not get any tidings, like a hero of faith. When I first met Jo in Dachau, I was shocked. He was horribly thin. He came to Dachau from the Amersfoort camp, and had already suffered much there. When he was taken into custody, his wife Thelma, the object of all his love, was seriously ill. How he longed for the news about her which was always intercepted. He did indeed give it all into the hands of the Lord, but he continued to long and hope, and the uncertainty continued to plague him. Tenderly and lovingly he would speak of her, and would open that heart of his with its great capacity for love. He constantly thought about his children. It was remarkable that he thought so much about his own childhood and his mother.

To this mental suffering was added physical suffering. He who needed so much food would suffer such terrible hunger. Not that he complained, indeed not! He bore it patiently in the power of Christ. But it simply broke his strength down day by day. And how painful his wounds were, his hands so broken up that he groaned in pain when he made up his bed, even though he could not. His feet were broken open and full of festering sores so that he could hardly walk. Yet four times a day he had to walk to the plantation where he worked. Soon he could no longer do that work. Thus Jo slowly but surely deteriorated.

And this tall young man surely had his share of physical abuse. He so easily drew attention, especially because of his height. He

---

[27] The Author is referring to the Liberation of 1944. —Editor.

was often beaten so that his wounds not only failed to heal, but actually increased. But he did not complain. He believed and bore it.

Of that camp-egoism that always said, "If I only get my share," Jo had none. He did not live for himself; he lived for others. One evening I happened to remark that I was so hungry. He said nothing. However, when we were in bed, he came to me and brought me half of his portion. He always took his bread to eat in bed so that he would not lie awake of hunger. Of this bread he offered me a share. But I refused it, for I knew he needed it worse than I. He persisted that I must accept it and not cause him sadness by refusal. Though I refused, he continued persisting. And thus I had to take it from a man who himself was suffering such hunger. That was Jo Kapteyn for you. He was that way in everything.

Jo remained very clear and vigorous of spirit. We often talked with each other in Block 28. I especially recall our conversations about prayer. This was a subject, of course, with which we were thrown into contact every day in the concentration camp. The discussion ran about the question of how we must pray. I can still hear him say that we must not pray with a persistent whining to God, as a little child does about something that he insists upon having. In harmony with this, it was also his purpose to write a book on prayer if he would ever come out of the concentration camp alive; a book in accordance with the insight that he had received on the subject in the camp experience.

This conversation had a peculiar consequence. We could not always agree on the subject of prayer, more especially on this point of spoiled persistence. To my mind the occasion for this difference lay in our different perception of Mark 11:22-24, especially verse 24, "Therefore I say to you, whatever things you ask when you pray, believe that you receive them, and you will have them." It concerned specifically our praying for deliverance from our imprisonment. He was deathly afraid to be carnal in these prayers. This he called "whining" to God. In this respect I was, of course, in full agreement with him, and I also saw this danger very clearly. Yet there was a difference between us. But what was it exactly? At first I thought that I was advanced a step further in my conception of prayer than he was. For me it was an unshaken conviction that I would come out of the camp alive. He did not have that feeling. I was convinced and I really believed that I would also receive that which I desired in my prayer. He hesitated on this point. Was this unbelief on his part?

After we had lain in bed for a while that evening, he came to me for a moment to talk. He said, "I believe that you are right after all, and I have perfect repose. Tell Thelma that all is well, whatever God does, and that I always have thought of her with the greatest love. And I believe that I also may advance as far as you have attained." Moved to tears, we pressed each other's hands. That was shortly before his death. When I last saw him, I knew why he had hesitated. It was the same for both of us. We were, after all, fully agreed. And yet neither of us realized it at that time.

We also spoke much together about the situation in the Reformed (*Gereformeerd*) Churches. We were convinced that sooner or later a schism would take place and that we would be cast out. What a prophetic illumination he had in this respect as well.

But his end was drawing near. His efforts to be received into the hospital for his wounds failed twice. They chased him away like a mangy dog. By this they really murdered him. Humanly speaking, there would have been a possibility of recovery if they had admitted him into the hospital on time. At last he could not go on. He tried once more to gain admittance. I can still see him as he stumbled his way to the roll call when the call sounded out: "All applicants out!" He was *one devoted unto death*. He was also *one ready to die*. When I saw this hero of faith, in whom the life of the old heroes was powerfully present, stagger away, I understood at last the meaning of his *hesitation*. It was not the hesitation of a man who had not yet progressed as far as I had, as I had first thought, but the hesitation of a man whose feet were treading a *different path* than I was. His feet were on the road of death; mine were on the road to life. Then I understood that the Lord had withheld from him what He had not withheld from me: *the confidence to pray that petition as I had*. And that because his time was fulfilled and mine was not. His calling on earth was finished, and it was his time to be reaped. He had to enter into the fulfilment of his calling in heaven. Indeed, the harvest that is ready does not call to be left on the field, but calls for the sickle of the reaper. A ripe harvest would have no value remaining on the field, for it has no purpose there. A new occupation calls to it. It calls for that new occupation when it calls for the sickle of the reaper. Thus it was with Jo Kapteyn. In his calling here, he had become a ripe harvest on earth; why should he remain here any longer? And so he called for the privilege to enter into his new calling, namely, to be a soul under the altar. He called for the Lord of the harvest, "Come Lord Jesus, yes, come quickly." Therefore the Author of prayer, the Holy Spirit, did not work in him the prayer of faith to remain alive, because there was in the wise council of the Lord of the harvest no possibility for such a life on earth any more. And thus Jo was right when he spoke of not using persistent whining in our prayers. It applied to himself more than he realized. For him who was being led, and to that end, it would indeed have been whining, grieving and resisting the Holy Spirit. Through his faith, this man on his way to his death was wholly beyond this sin. So his hesitation was not weakness and unbelief, but the faith and obedience of the child who may not annoyingly clamour around his Father's feet. It was a matter of not approaching where he might not approach — and so he did not desire it either. His hour had come. And he loved not his life unto death, but he was faithful even unto death. That evening he was admitted into the hospital. I had seen Jo for the last time. A few days later he died, shortly before I myself was taken to the hospital.

He had gone to his Home where all prayer-struggles are solved in eternal worship and joyous "Hallelujahs!" He had gone home to Him of whom he wrote that fine book, *Die is en Die was en Die Komt* (Which is and Which Was and Which is to Come).

Jo left me a good inheritance. In our conversations we often spoke about the future of our church and people. How clearly this prophet saw this future. He was convinced that after the war, which he believed Germany would surely lose, a mighty struggle would be awaiting us, a struggle against National Socialism, a struggle also against a false unity-movement which would stand under the influence of this National Socialism.

He saw that the battle would have to be fought in the sphere of *church*, *state*, and *society*. He foresaw that for anyone who would wage this battle in true obedience to the Scriptures, *isolation* would be necessary. How deeply was he filled with anxious concern for our Reformed (*Gereformeerd*) Churches, in which he also saw the spiritual and moral decay revealing itself, and conformity to the world growing on every side! How he saw the difficulties which Christian education would have to face, and Christian political action, Christian social action, and more of such. And I shared this fear with him. So we agreed that we would have to assume this struggle and would have to call others to the struggle. According to this promise I began to act after my return. And I hope by the enabling grace of God to continue in it in the future. When I returned, I soon perceived — when I began to find my bearings again — that this prophet had not only been correct in his predictions, but that the decay had already gone further than we had been conscious of. In church and state and society a national infiltration had already taken place that foreboded the worst. May God grant that many who desire to live by the Word may see it, and may sharpen their weapons to combat this spirit of the times, wherever it has gained a foot-hold. For National Socialism is not *dead*. It is *alive*. It merely bears another name now.

But to return to our story, as I said before, I was also committed to the hospital, that murder-den. I remained there from August 26, 1942, until October 10, 1942. Would they also use me for a guinea-pig? Indeed they did. Twice they experimented with me. What I did not know at the time later became evident: It was a harmless test. The injections they gave me were merely pure water for the purpose of testing the assimilation of water by the human body. But a general nervousness overpowered us whenever our names were read for these experiments.

That I did not die in the hospital is a miracle of God. No one did a thing for the high fevers I had. They simply let me lie. But I never had an unbroken day. For every little thing they would get me out of bed. For example, they would give me blood tests. I shivered and shook from fever and cold, for I lay practically naked, and would have to walk through a long stone passage where the most horrible draft struck me, and then I would stand on my bare feet for an hour before my turn came. The next day the same thing was undergone again for the sake of being x-rayed. To this day I do not know how I, too weak to even stand, was able to come through such an hour of standing. But the Nazis, with their mania for statistics, worried very little whether their patient died or not. There were still plenty of others with whom to tamper.

I had been in the hospital for a whole month when the doctor came into my room and by my bed for the first time. This was also the first time I received medicine. At that time I received eight tablets at once. But experience had taught me that they would probably be better for the toilet than for my stomach and so directly into the toilet they went.

The nursing left much to be desired, of course. This was done by unschooled personnel, because the trained were all prisoners. Only an occasional sanitarian was found among them. Of course, you had to make your own bed and clean your own room. There was no strengthening food. It was all the same camp diet, cabbage-soup. Only stomach patients got a light diet. So, naturally, the death rate was terribly high.

My eye-trouble also started in this hospital. They simply paid no attention to my request to go to the eye-clinic for an examination. The pain became more violent by the day. At last my right eye was completely blind. About a year later I was sent to an academic eye-clinic in München. But by then it was already too late. As the result of the hunger suffered in the camp, my eye had become incurably blind.

On October 10, 1942, I dismissed myself from the hospital, even though I was far from cured. The nurse told me that, in order to make room in the ward, they were about to gather up a load of patients to be gassed. It seemed best to me to slip out of this if possible. So I returned to Block 28 on October 10, and after a week of being "excused" I was again put in the labour commando for road-building. But I was too weak for this work, and contrived to have my boss dismiss me again. From this time on a more lenient camp-administration began to dawn. After this I worked in a commando called "*Wildpark*," in a gravel-pit. This was also too heavy. This was during a time that we were permitted to receive packages of food and clothing. With a little tin of artificial honey, I got my dismissal from the boss. He would see to it that I got into an easier commando. A few more items from my gift package fixed this up for me. He got me into the mattress commando. But my eye ailment also made this work impossible for me, so I looked for another job. I managed to keep myself enrolled in the mattress commando, so that I did not appear in the books as being without work, and thus be pushed into a heavy commando again, or into the Invalid Block. So I remained in the mattress department, and did all kinds of little odd-jobs. Later I became a kind of boss and still later a ward-boss. That was the end of heavy work for me, and at times the end of all work.

Since we were officially permitted, after December 1942, to receive packages of food, I began, through the loving concern of many in the fatherland, to recover some strength. My weight began to build up, and I could feel my strength returning. I passed unharmed through the violent typhoid epidemic that struck the camp in the spring of 1943. Of course, there were still difficult days. The thumb-screws were often tightened unexpectedly. But in general the conditions were much better. A new camp command forbade physical maltreatment at the hand of fellow-prisoners. We all breathed more freely. If things might remain this way, then we would have the possibility, even though it was always imprisonment, to hold out until the end of the war. Graciously the Lord heard our prayers and lightened our burdens. Hope grew by the day. The radio-reports which came through to us gave new courage. The end appeared to come into sight. However, I did not have to stay to wait for that end. Unexpectedly, I was dismissed.

14. Dachau, the World of Contrasts

Dachau was also a world of the most sharp opposites, also between nationalities. There were representatives of all peoples of Europe. There were Russians, Poles, Czechs, Frenchmen, Luxembourgers, Grecians, Croats, Hungarians, Italians, Belgians, Yugoslavs, Austrians, Germans, Danes, Norwegians, and Dutch. A very international company, you see. And yet the contrast between the various races would often appear in a most striking manner. Whoever thinks that this communal suffering will also naturally cause a bond of comradeship to grow is sadly mistaken. All that there was to this comradeship were the bombastic speeches that we had to hear from time to time.

The Poles, for example, who in general had to bear a heavy share of the affliction, were quite badly knocked off their bearings. This often revealed itself in a most passionate manner. The hunger which they suffered made them very selfish and grabby, so that they could hardly wish anything good to others. When they had something that they had "organized" and were devouring it, they could very comfortably observe that others looked on with hungry eyes, or even asked for a bit to still the hunger. They did not think about sharing any of it. I will not claim that all were so, but the greater part of the Polish Block, where I stayed, was exactly that way. This occasionally raised painful conflicts. There was a peculiar opposition between the Poles and the Dutch. They kept us at a distance and thoroughly ignored us. I did not understand exactly what caused this, so I tried to find out. And I did find out. It was plain that they took us as half-Germans. Our speech already gave this idea. Hence they trusted us as little as they did the Germans, and would have nothing to do with us. For them, a German was like a red object to a steer. No wonder! They had experienced very little good from the Germans. The contrast between the Poles and the Dutch was very unpleasant, and it made things very difficult for us.

This opposition also existed between other nationalities and the Germans.

You sometimes hear it said that there are also good Germans. Well, I did not see much of it in Dachau. If there are good Germans, there are probably no more than one in a million.

Even the German prisoners in the camp were, almost without exception, possessed by the world-conquering frenzy of Germany. When we came into contact with a German in the concentration camp, it was ten to one that he would begin to harp about Germany, where *the* culture is found, *the* science, *the* art, *the* industry, *the* everything. And then that miserable German character would so typically appear: cruelty and sentimentality — cruelty that would spare nothing and no one, and sentimentality that was nauseating

— side by side. In the same five minutes this German fellow-prisoner was a brute who ruled over you and a flatterer who would lick your hand. No, indeed, a German never belies his true nature. Add to this their untrustworthiness. We could never depend on their word. If they could cheat us, they would not miss the chance. Therefore we avoided them as much as we possibly could.

The German Communists were especially notorious. Since they were the oldest prisoners, they held the highest posts in the camp. The camp-bosses, the block-bosses and ward-bosses, and the secretaries were German Communists. They bowed and crawled before the S.S., and, to gain a little of the good graces of the S.S., they would abuse their fellow prisoners, especially the clergy, in the most cruel manner. *They have many murders on their conscience.*

On December 19, 1942, we Dutch clergy, along with the Czech and Luxembourg clergy, were brought from Block 28, where the Polish clergy were kept, to Block 26, where the German clergy were. The total number of clergy in Dachau were approximately eleven hundred. I was not greatly pleased with this change. Here I met the Roman Catholic and Protestant clergy of Germany. What a disappointment this meeting and acquaintance with the Protestant German pastors was. In The Netherlands we had read much about the heroic struggle of the German evangelical pastors against the Nazis. We had harboured admiration and gratitude for this struggle. My contact with these men made it necessary for me to thoroughly revise my evaluation of this struggle. The image we had received of them was all too flattering, for they proved to be Germans like all the other Germans in the camp. I had thought I would meet men of principle, but they were not. With a rare exception, they were weaklings, brimful of German haughtiness. They despised everything that was not German, and not the least, us Dutchmen. They fully approved of what Hitler had done with The Netherlands. There was no trace whatsoever of a Christian consciousness of guilt and confession, except for one solitary exception whom I knew.

If this outfit of haughty, conceited German pastors was a picture of the men of the German Evangelical Church who put up a resistance on principle, then what must the rest have been who did not end up in a concentration camp?

They hoped that Hitler, that is, Germany, would win the war, without considering at all that this would mean the downfall of the church in Germany. To them, the German state was superior to the German church. Some of them even wrote a request to Hitler, asking to be taken into the German army, and a few even became members of the S.S. Often I had disputes with them in which they assumed such lofty attitudes that I could hardly restrain myself. At last I kept away from them, and also from their religious services. I never partook of what they called their Lord's Supper — which it was not. I could have no fellowship of faith with people who, against better knowledge, assumed responsibility for the Nazi misdeeds against the land and people and church of The Netherlands. Thus, how could there be a basis for communal prayers and songs?

To be honest, I must confess that the German Roman Catholic clergy were much more manly, and had a much more disapproving attitude towards the misdeeds of the Hitler regime. They, at least, showed much more understanding for nationalities other than German.

The contrast between the different prisoners was also very great. It almost seems impossible to wholly eliminate from human society or association the existence of rank or caste. At least they were even found in the concentration camp. Thus there were persons of rank and social standing who placed themselves high above the lower people. There were people of prominence and there were people of low rank, common prisoners and slaves. This was not the case of rank and caste as they had been developed in free society, which, though altogether unnecessary, had set themselves against the common people, those, namely, of the wealthy class, the cultured, those of rank and position. In that respect, we were indeed all alike, whatever we might have been in our former free society. In that respect we were now all slaves of the Third Reich. No, but in the camp, a caste developed of men-of-long-camp-service. Many of these profited at the expense of their fellow prisoners by robbing them. They became well-fed and fat, while their subordinates became more and more emaciated, and they looked on with perfect repose. I had a ward-boss in Block 28 who skimmed the little fat off the soup plates of his fellow prisoners, and stole bread out of their lockers for his own consumption.

And there was more of that nature. In any event, this contrast created an atmosphere of spite and revenge against all who held a high place.

Finally, there was in Dachau also a sharp contrast between *faith* and *unbelief*. Dachau was, in the last analysis, a city of total heathendom. It was an inferno of godlessness. Not even the slightest elements of a Christian style of life were to be found there. The throne of Satan stood in Dachau.

Never in my life have I heard such terrible blasphemies as there. Never have I experienced the commonness of cursing and swearing as there, and that by people who in terrible suffering lived on the very edge of the grave, and might expect to be called before the righteous Judge of heaven and earth at any moment.

This godlessness revealed itself in a passionate hatred for the Church, Christendom, and all things spiritual. The clergy especially had much to endure because of their faith.

For our faith we were cursed, raved at, and mistreated. The German Communists told us that the Nazis were altogether too pampering in the way they managed us. If they themselves could only come to power, then we would really experience something. Then we would again see the introduction of the stake, and they would dance around it as we stood in the flames.

Twice I had to give an account of the hope in me before the S.S. men, as a spectacle to the world and to angels and to men. The first time was out on the street shortly after I arrived in Dachau. I had just finished a little chore with a few fellow prisoners, and we were going back to our block. On the way we met a work-boss, who immediately saw by our high numbers that we were fresh arrivals. He accosted us and asked why we had been taken into custody. When it was my turn, I told him that it was because I was unwilling to promise not to pray for our queen. Immediately I received a full volley of mean curses, while Her Majesty also got her share. He asked if there was any other cause. I told him that I had delivered a sermon on the third chapter of Daniel, and particularly on the answers of the three young men to Nebuchad-nezzar, for which they were cast into the deep furnace. Then all his hatred against God and His people broke out in the most blasphemous language, matched with appropriate curses directed at me. It was a theatre in Dachau.

The second time was towards Christmas, 1942. I was called to appear before an S.S. block-boss. He asked me to explain the well-known Christmas song, *Es Ist Ein Ros' Entsprungen* (Lo, How a Rose E'er Blooming). Then I also witnessed the same outburst of hatred and godlessness. A theatre in Dachau, indeed! Thus Dachau was a world of the sharpest contrasts, which did not make life very easy, but rather increased the tensions.

15. Dachau as a Place in Which the Holy Spirit Worked

What I am about to write now is really the most important part of what I have to tell about my stay in the concentration camp of Dachau. All the horrors that I have pictured for you — and I have not told all, but only a snatch here and there — you may forget. But that which I am about to narrate now may not be surrendered to oblivion. For these are "the praises of the LORD and His strength and His wonderful works that He has done . . ." I must tell them so "that the generation to come might know them, the children who would be born, that they may arise and declare them to their children, that they may set their hope in God and not forget the works of God, but keep His commandments; and may not be like their fathers, a stubborn and rebellious generation, a generation that did not set its heart aright and whose spirit was not faithful to God" (Ps. 78:4b-8).

Indeed, in Dachau the God of all grace did wonders of grace by His Word and Spirit every day. Oh, it was indeed a dreadful time for me that I spent there, and yet it is not at all a hollow phrase when I say that I would for no amount of money have missed this time of my life, since it was so unspeakably rich in grace. I saw God there. The LORD was in this place. It was a house of God and a gate of heaven.

Behold, both joy and light
Will dawn for the upright.[28]

---

[28] Psalm 97:6b (*Book of Praise*).

Yes, much joy and much light.

Perhaps the urge might arise in someone's heart as he reads of all the suffering and tortures, to pity me. I beg you, do not pity me. For one, to whom the Lord has shown so much purifying, sanctifying, encouraging, comforting, and sustaining grace, is not to be pitied, but rather to be envied. If the great word *martyr* should rise to your lips, I beg you do not utter it; restrain it. To be a martyr is truly more than this.

It is — I can say this without any pathos — it is an unspeakable privilege, a great unmerited favour, to have been in Dachau, to have been a theatre to the world and to angels and to men.

Of this gracious work of the Holy Spirit wrought through the Word of God for me, I shall now tell something. I desire to do that in the sober style of Psalm 66, "Come and hear, all you who fear God; and I will declare what He has done for my soul" (Ps. 66:16).

In all kinds of ways they tried to crush to death and rub out the life of faith. The battle of the Nazis, the historical conflict pictured in Psalm 2, was in its deepest sense directed against the Lord and against His Anointed. They tried to strike the Lord and His Anointed through those who confessed Him. Therefore, it was officially forbidden to speak about religious things in the camp. In our letters we might not even quote Bible texts. Nevertheless, we naturally did speak with others in the camp about the only Name given under heaven among men, and we testified about Jesus Christ whenever we had the opportunity. For we must obey God rather than men.

As a means to root out our life of faith, the rule that we might not keep our Bibles was also enforced. They were taken away from us. Dachau had to be a city without God and without His Word. Only after the fall of Stalingrad did we again receive our Bibles. The Germans, afraid that Providence would also be against them, apparently became superstitious.

Being deprived of my Bible was a heavy cross to bear. What riches of comfort I had received out of that Book during my stay in prison! It had been a fountain of strength to me! How the Holy Spirit had strengthened my faith by means of the Word! For there is, of course, no more restful living than in company with, and by the guidance of, the Word. Every day anew my hunger and thirst was to have my faith strengthened through the work of the Spirit by means of the Holy Gospel. But now I did not have a Bible anymore. How I missed it! Thus through this lack of the Bible, I was, as far as the Word of God was concerned, compelled to depend wholly on my *memory*. Never was I so glad that in my youth my parents made me memorize so many passages, Psalms, songs, and hymns. I often grumbled about it at that time, of course. But now I experienced the blessing of it all. But naturally, much of what I had then learned had sunk away below the threshold of my consciousness.

In the morning when I stood for roll call, I had a few moments' time to pray my morning prayer for the day that had once more dawned. I asked my God to bring to my recollection the particular passage of His Word that I would have need of for the new day. And He always heard that prayer. I discovered something very remarkable in this connection: The verses of Scripture that arose in my recollection were mostly words that dealt with liberation, sparing of life, and future tasks, without my really thinking purposely about such a thing.

Now someone will say that such a thing is not at all remarkable, the wish was simply father to the thought. However, anyone who has known our life in the camp would not expect such an opinion. Naturally, I hoped for liberation and prayed for it, and naturally, I hoped for a future task and also prayed for that. But that was not the thing that controlled all my considerations. *That* was only *resignation* to the Lord. However much I longed to return to my task in the Church of the Lord, yet the whole of this desire stood under the discipline of the resignation to the Lord. "Not my will, but Thy will be done," was the principle that controlled me. All that God would do would be good for me.

In that spiritual frame of mind, of complete resignation, the Lord frequently spoke His Word of liberation and calling. That drew my attention. But at the same time it made me afraid. Recollecting such texts made me afraid that I would also fall into that text-Christianity which does not live by the Word, but by such texts as flash to the mind and exactly fit the bill. Had I not testified against that so often in my preaching? And so, in my perplexity, I also made this a matter of prayer, and asked the Lord that He might instruct me in this situation, and make it plain to me that I might, indeed, hold as firm and settled such words of recollection. For I desired nothing but to be well-pleasing to the Lord in all things. By constant prayer, it also became plain to me that in my case the situation was altogether different from that of those other people. For those leaning towards text-Christianity have Moses and the prophets. They are not limited and assigned to such suddenly striking texts. Their desire to have their information from such a source, while they have their Bible, is self-willed religion and sinful speculation, which is condemned by the Scriptures. But I had been deprived of my Bible by force, so that I was wholly limited by and dependent on my memory, and therefore I might freely plead upon God's own promises regarding the work of the Holy Spirit that would bring all things to our memory. That promised Comforter would in this do His promised work.

When I had arrived at this point, I could appreciate with a thankful heart what the Holy Spirit brought to my recollection out of the Scriptures, so that I believingly lived, not by a word or two, but by The Word. In that way the Holy Spirit, through the Word, strengthened my life every day, so that sufficient to each day was the grace thereof, and I could continue my way every day with gladness. Therefore I have never known one day of wavering, not even in the deepest depths and the blackest night of my grief. His song and my prayer to the God of my life were always with me:

> *But the LORD will send salvation,*
> *And by day His love provide.*
> *He shall be my exultation,*
> *And my song at eventide.*
> *On His praise e'en in the night*
> *I will ponder with delight,*
> *And in prayer, transcending distance,*
> *Seek the God of my existence.*[29]

---

[29] Psalm 42:5 (*Book of Praise*).

Never have I understood so well that word of James: "My brethren, count it all joy when you fall into various trials" (James 1:2). Pure joy it was.

For Thou hast been my God forever.
Let Thy good Spirit guide my feet.[30]

And it was a place of pure joy.

But there is something else in which the work of the Holy Spirit manifested itself by the Word. And that was that He purified my faith by this service of testings. What the flail on the threshing-floor means for the wheat, and what the fires in the smelters mean to the gold, and what the cutting and polishing means to the diamond, that the testings by means of the Spirit and the Word meant for my faith. It meant the removal of the dross to bring to light the pure, finished product. By that process it showed itself as pure, genuine faith, genuine faith which has but *one point of support*, namely, *God*, to be left only with God, and therefore, to find support only in His Word. Not the Word plus all kinds of pious words, but *only* God and His Word.

That faith was strong. So strong that I could sing,

With Thee I crush a troop and conquer all,
And with my God I scale the highest wall.[31]

Not with God plus ladders and ropes, or with God plus swords and spears, but with God *through faith*.

The hope of faith shall not deceive us;
The Saviour's words are true and sure.[32]

Then I also saw so clearly what the experience of faith really is. It is something altogether different from a self-willed, flattering construction that sets man in the centre. This is not it at all. The

---

[30] Psalm 143:5 (*Book of Praise*).
[31] Psalm 18:9b (*Book of Praise*).
[32] Hymn 53:1a (*Book of Praise*).

experience of faith is deadly sober, of a child-like simplicity, in which God is the centre, by which the child lays his little hand in the Father's large hand and says, "My Father, Thou dost not lie; Thy Word is truth; Thy promises, as many as there are, are all yes and amen."

Indeed, was not Dachau the laboratory of the Holy Spirit?

In still another respect it was such a laboratory, namely, in that He gave rise to such a rich life of prayer. For, properly speaking, prayer in Dachau was praying without ceasing. Life was praying, praying was life. Life was *constantly being occupied* day and night with God. And prayer had expanding room. It seemed as if one prayed through the open door of heaven and into the Father-heart of God. Thus the Holy Spirit, by means of the Word, wrought the prayer of faith. In that prayer, the Holy Spirit prays along; indeed, God called to God. And He that searches out knew what was the mind of the Spirit, because He makes intercession for the saints according to the will of God. Hence, the marvel of those often striking answers to prayer.

Let me describe a few of them to you, to the praise of God's grace.

In the beginning I was more or less lonely in Dachau. I do not mean lonely as far as God is concerned, but with respect to men. I had no companionship, because I was the only Dutchman in the block. But man is a social being. He needs to be able to exchange thoughts with like-minded people. So I had need of a person with whom I could speak of the riches of God's grace, of the Fountain of strength and comfort residing in the Gospel, of the wonders which the Lord was performing. But I had no one. I thought of Paul, who was comforted by the coming of Titus; this lowly man, Paul, before the God who comforts the lowly. Therefore I made my loneliness for man a matter of prayer. I prayed, "Lord, give me a person with whom I can find contact and with whom I can speak about Thee and Thy Word."

Now in another concentration camp far from Dachau, there was another man who was lonesome just as I was. He also prayed a prayer and said the same thing that I had. Behold the wonderful answer to prayer! On a certain morning when I had reported at

Liebhof for labour with the commando, I noticed a new-comer in the group. He looked at me and I looked at him. But I did not immediately recognize him. He was not only incorporated into my commando, but even into my subdivision. We spoke to one another, and sure enough, he was a Dutchman, and also a Reformed (*Gereformeerd*) minister. He was a colleague of mine, Jannes Van Raalte.

So this was the man for whose coming I had prayed! And he who had then been imprisoned in Buchenwald felt that I was the man for whom he had prayed. God had heard the prayers of both and had brought him over to Dachau. That was a miracle of answered prayer. Not only this, but also that he was assigned to the same labour commando and subdivision in which I was placed. How else could I have found him in those twenty-two thousand men? Thus the Lord brought us together. And, oh, how much we profited from each other! We became faithful friends bound more closely than by ties of blood. It was a glorious time. Our life together was a spiritual feast. And when we worked together there in the burning sun or the torrents of rain, how gloriously we spoke together of the riches of the Scriptures. We prayed together under the blue dome of the heavens for the Church, our country and people, and the royal family. We prayed for the power of faith, that we might carry our cross joyfully. Together we sang our Psalms. We tried to keep each other alive. And so the days became nothing less than feast-days. Later, more colleagues came to Dachau, both from the Reformed (*Gereformeerd*) Churches in The Netherlands and the Dutch Reformed (*Hervormd*) Church. There were Rev. Kapteyn, Dr. Sietsma, Rev. Tunderman, Rev. Overduin, Rev. Idema, Rev. Guillaume, Rev. Smilde, Rev. Hinloopen, Rev. Krop, Rev. Padt, Rev. Den Hartog, Rev. Zwiep, Rev. De Geus, and Rev. Bouman.

The time spent with Jannes Van Raalte on *Liebhof* belongs to the most pleasant of the times I had in Dachau, and is unforgettable. Jannes and I remained together until we were both taken into the hospital, I first and he later. From then on, our ways in the labour commando parted, but God had comforted us by bringing us together in answer to our prayers. It was as the Psalm says,

To God, who hears our supplication,
We come to pay our vow;
Soon men from every tribe and nation
Before our God shall bow.[33]

In that terrible year of famine of 1942, in the month of July, it was dreadful even for Dachau. We were fast going to pieces, and walked around with death in our shoes. Our feet were swollen; festering sores tortured us; our hunger plagued us the whole day without letup.

Oh, that hunger! You know that we have proverbial expressions for all kinds of occasions and experiences; they are such convenient devices, so easy to handle, especially when one is not involved in that of which the proverb speaks. Someone has compared them to stilts. And so, calmly and without any emotion, we also bring out that proverb about hunger. We say, "Hunger is a sharp sword." Do you *know* that? Do you *know* how sharp a sword hunger is? Do you know that it cuts asunder all moral and spiritual bonds without scruples, that it turns men into robbers and murderers, so that they only listen to the one command of their hungry stomach, which says, "*Take*?" Do you *know* that, you proverb-quoting man, who do not experience hunger? Do you know that this hunger which drags man down so low knows no respect of persons? Do not swell your chest and say, "It would never happen to me, that I would rob my fellow-men to have something to eat." For I warn you, that if you do not struggle against it by faith, you will surely do it. For a really hungry man, there is no fellow-man. For him there is only *himself*. He must live, and he must eat. There is still something left. That is the last, perhaps, and it may belong to a friend, a brother, a husband, a wife, or child — *take* it and *eat*. For *I* must live! It is the daily struggle of the hungry one not to become a predatory animal. And I have known many men of high standing put forth all their power to remain standing in that awful struggle to remain human. And I have seen them give up the struggle and fall. Do not judge them too harshly. It was so difficult and so terrible. He who thinks to stand, take heed lest he fall!

---

[33] Psalm 65:1b (*Book of Praise*).

On a morning of July 1942, I discovered, to my consternation, that the little piece of bread I had saved in my locker, which I had been so careful with, was *stolen*. That was at four in the morning, and I would not get food again until eleven-thirty. My stomach cried out for food. One has to experience this to know what a depth of hatred and temptation such a thing opens before you.

When I came to *Liebhof* in the morning, I told Jannes. But he could not help me, for he himself had nothing. We discussed the situation together. What to do? In this misery there was only one way out: turn to God. We said to each other, "We are going to tell our Father. For our heavenly Father has given us a message about our food and clothing and shelter, and the Saviour has told us, 'For your heavenly Father knows that you need all these things' " (Matt. 6:32). Now it was also necessary for us to believe in childlike faith on His Word. This heavenly Father is Lord of heaven and earth and therefore also has command over food and clothing and shelter. To Him we would appeal, this God who *gives* to the beasts their food and to the young ravens when they cry. How much rather will He not give to His children in need, who in faith stretch out their empty hands to Him, and plead, "Father, give to us if it pleases Thee."

So Jannes and I laid the question of the stolen bread before our heavenly Father and waited, trusting in His great power.

> *Our God, the* Lord, *is strong to save*
> *From mortal danger, from the grave*
> *And every cruel oppression.*[34]

It must have been about half an hour after our prayer that I heard my boss, a man who despised God and His cause, and also His servants, calling my name across the field, "Where is that *Knopp*?"

I answered and said, "Here I am." I wonder what's up now? I thought. For when such unexpected developments occur, one always expected the very worst in a concentration camp.

He called, "*Knopp*, come here a minute."

---

[34] Psalm 68:8c (*Book of Praise*).

I came, and to my amazement he asked, "*Knopp*, would you perhaps be able to make use of a piece of bread? I had a piece to spare this morning and have kept it for you."

O God, how great are Thy works towards us! Here was a miracle of answered prayer. This prayer of faith was marvellously heard. And then I laughed aloud, a childlike laugh of faith. I thought of Revelation 12, which tells us that the earth came to the rescue of the woman who had fled into the wilderness. That is what happened here. Then I told my boss, "Man, you won't believe this, but I tell you that your giving me this piece of bread is a miracle of answered prayer." Then I went on and told him the sad story of the stolen bread, and I also told him of our prayer to God about it. I told him that God had used him to keep one of His children from starvation.

He said, "Nice joke," and laughed. It was a laugh of unbelief that had no eye for the miracles of the God of Elijah, the God who also lives today.

Whoever has experienced such a thing from his heavenly Father can never forget it. The devoted offering up of his whole life is the least that he can give to his heavenly Father. Together Jannes and I thanked the Lord and sang:

> *O bless the LORD, my soul, bless your Preserver;*
> *Let all within me praise His Name with fervour.*
> *My soul, forget not all His benefits;*
> *O bless the LORD, who pardons your transgression,*
> *Who heals your illnesses in His compassion,*
> *Who saves you and redeems you from the Pit.*[35]

The beginning of August 1942 came. A package of food came for Rev. Van Raalte. Now the sending of food-packages was strictly forbidden, but his wife had decided to take the risk and try it. It was surely a festive message which came to him that a package had arrived for him. Try to imagine in our barren and hopelessly starved existence, a package of good old Dutch butter and cheese. But, alas, it was not as festive as all that. For the hardened camp-commander added the information that the package would not be

---

[35] Psalm 103:1 (*Book of Praise*).

forwarded to him. He was going to distribute the contents among the weaker patients in the hospital.

So it was presented. The naked truth was, of course, that those illustrious S.S. guards would use it for their own advantage. Oh, how deep and bitter was our disappointment!

Barely a ray of light had fallen into our dark night before it was again extinguished. This made the night of our hunger even darker than before.

We asked ourselves, "What can God's purpose be with this?" Did He mean to tell us that we must prepare ourselves to perish of hunger? Perhaps that was the meaning. We did not know.

Or did He mean to test our faith, which is more precious even than gold, which, though perishable stuff, must be tested by fire? Was it in order that the trying of our faith might be for praise and glory and honour in the revelation of Jesus Christ?

Did it mean that in this way we would obtain the object of our faith, the salvation of our souls? Did He desire to demonstrate through us and our misery, that man must place his trust and confidence in nothing else, in no other creature, but in Him alone? Or was His purpose that we should ask Him, who had sustained His servant Elijah alive at the Brook Cherith by means of ravens, that we should ask Him to incline the heart of the unmerciful camp commander to mercy and compassion, so that He would use this enemy of His Name for the preservation of our lives, as He did in the case of Elijah, with dumb fowls of the air? For were we not His children and also His servants?

We did not know. But we were sure that God meant to teach us something through this disappointment.

So we brought our problem and our perplexity to our Father in heaven, and said, "Lord, show us Thy ways, make plain to us Thy paths."

But nothing happened. No answer came. Or rather, we received an answer that really increased the difficulty. For in that same week I also received word that a package of food had come for me, but that it would not be forwarded to me.

Was that the answer to our prayers? Did the answer mean that it was according to His omnipotent power and all-wise counsel that we should perish of hunger? Or did it mean that He desired to see us completely resign our food-packages, so that He alone would be our trust and stay? Did it mean that we must pray for the softening of the hard heart of the camp commander? Or did it mean the one as well as the other, namely, that we should continue to believe, regardless of which way our fortune turned? That by believing, in hope against hope that He would sustain us alive? That we had to let go of our food-packages? That our God would soften the hard heart? We struggled in prayer and *continued to believe*.

He alone remained for us. So we were in Dachau, a theatre to the world and to angels and to men.

No more did we speak about our food-packages. They were gone, as far as we were concerned. We had yielded them completely to the Lord.

Several days later we were both called up to appear at the office of the camp commander. *And there both of our packages were handed to us.* Dutch butter, Dutch cheese, and some other tidbits. And then we really wept like little children, so glad were we and so deeply moved.

> *It seemed a dream to us, and we*
> *All laughed and shouted joyfully . . .*
> *The LORD has done great things for us;*
> *With joy and thanks His Name we bless.*[36]

Never have I eaten my bread from the hand of my heavenly Father as directly as I did then. On the way back to our block we already began to sample a little of it. We could hardly restrain ourselves.

> *Forever blest be God, my Saviour,*
> *Who has not turned away my prayer,*
> *Nor has withheld from me His mercy,*
> *His never-failing love and care.*[37]

And thus Dachau was the working place of the Holy Spirit.

---

[36] Psalm 126:1b, d (*Book of Praise*).
[37] Psalm 66:8b (*Book of Praise*).

Naturally, we also prayed for our liberation. But we prayed with this restriction, "Lord, Thou art also engaged in purifying us, and if this is not yet completed, then do not grant our desires. Let Thy will be done. If it pleases Thee, may our liberation come soon, for Thou dost know how we desire to return again, to be engaged in the proclamation of Thy Word, and how we long to be at home with those who are dear to us. Prepare us for that future task and send us when we are ready to be fruitful to Thee."

In my own personal prayer I added the petition, "O God, if it may please Thee, then glorify Thy name and power by causing the same hand that opened the doors to imprison me, now also to open it for my release."

This prayer the Lord was also graciously pleased to hear. Not that He released Jannes and myself at the same time. We had so ardently desired that, and had asked Him for that privilege. We, who had experienced so much joy and sorrow together, dreaded so much to be separated from each other; but God's ways are deep in wisdom, and Jannes was also permitted to return home, healthy and well, after Dachau was liberated by the Americans.

On October 9th, 1943, at seven in the morning, the block secretary came to me and said, "You are dismissed."

I became a little angry, and said, "Man, don't play a prank with such a thing."

But he persisted. It was not a prank or a joke, but the truth. "I knew it already last night," he said, "but I didn't want to tell you for fear that you would not be able to sleep."

I could not believe my ears. Could it really be true? Had the suffering after two years really come to its end? Had the prayers which were sent up at home and in the churches, and in so many families, even by little children, been heard at last? Would the Gestapo and the S.S. at last be compelled by the Lord to open to me the gates of freedom?

Yes, it was all true! With God, nothing is impossible. And oh, how glad I was that I could go at last. But at the same time, I felt very sad for those who had to stay behind, for we had experienced so much together, and how much more would they still have to undergo! If I could only take them with me!

Now I would be permitted to return to my family, and to my work which my God had once been pleased to entrust to me.

Now I would be able to administer the Word again, and labour for the purity of the Church. Thus I would work for the purity of my people also, for he who keeps the Church pure is serving the people, for he is preserving the purity of the people.

After a number of necessary routine details, I received my proof of release. I was free!

An S.S. man brought me from the camp to the station of Dachau. Then he left me. I was free! The doors of the past and the future opened to me again. I was living again. Living as a human being. The snare was broken, and I had escaped. The slave No. 29807 no longer existed. O Thou great, wise, almighty, and gracious God; Thou hast done this for me! Thou art the glory of our strength, and by Thy favour is our horn exalted.

After an uneventful trip, I arrived at the station in Rotterdam on Sunday morning at 11:48. What an unforgettable Sunday for me! I met my dear ones who had been separated from me for two years. My wife had been able to survive those two years through the heroic power of faith, as an example to many. In that respect as well, besides the many other ways, she had been a strong support to me. She was strong in God. How glad I was to see my congregation again! I still see the glad, beaming faces, and the tear-filled eyes as the congregation was dismissed that evening at Tidemanstraat.

> *Then it was said among the nations,*
> *"To them the* L'ORD *gave restoration."*
> *The* L'ORD *has done great things for us;*
> *With joy and thanks His Name we bless.*[38]

But the most wonderful of all was that Sunday afternoon. I had always hoped and prayed that I might return just before the celebration of the Lord's Supper. For I had missed it so during the two years of imprisonment. When I was dismissed on that Saturday, I thought, Tomorrow my congregation is celebrating the Lord's Supper, but I will be too late to be there.

But when by Saturday evening I had already arrived at Cologne, I took courage.

---

[38] Psalm 126:1b (*Book of Praise*).

140

So indeed it was that on that Sunday it was my privilege again, after two years, to remember the Lord's death.

On Sunday the 17th, I again preached for my congregation for the first time. When I mounted the pulpit I felt as though I had arisen from the dead. To avoid all sensation, I had desired that the fact that I would preach should not be made known.

I preached from Psalm 116:12-15, "What shall I render to the LORD for all His benefits towards me? I will take up the cup of salvation and call upon the name of the LORD. I will pay my vows to the LORD now in the presence of all His people. Precious in the sight of the LORD is the death of His saints."

So Dachau belonged to the past; a new calling lay before me. The theatre in Dachau to the world and to angels and to men was a thing of the past. May God grant that those spectators of the theatre will not accuse me, but that I may be found faithful in the eyes of Him who was the great Spectator, and who saw more than the world and angels and men, since He saw the heart.

Is it a wonder that in this heart the song echoed:

> *Now shall my heart sing praise to Thee:*
> *Gone is the grief that silenced me.*
> *I may, delivered from despair,*
> *Now laud Thy Name in song and prayer.*
> *Forever, LORD, my God and Saviour,*
> *Will I give thanks for Thy great favour.*[39]

For of Him and through Him and to Him are all things, to whom be glory forever.

---

[39] Psalm 30:7 (*Book of Praise*).

Epilogue

One question pressed upon me after I returned from Dachau. This question was not, "Why was I allowed to return?" I knew the answer to that: The Lord still had a task for me to complete. Otherwise I would have died like so many others. I was not yet ripe for the harvest. That answer was given me in Rev. 14:14-16:

"Then I looked, and behold, a white cloud, and on the cloud sat One like the Son of Man, having on His head a golden crown, and in His hand a sharp sickle. And another angel came out of the temple, crying with a loud voice to Him who sat on the cloud, 'Thrust in Thy sickle and reap; for the time has come for Thee to reap, for the harvest of the earth is ripe.' So He who sat on the cloud thrust in His sickle on the earth, and the earth was reaped."

However, the question that pressed upon me was, "Why did I have to come back at exactly *that time*?" It was at the time that the dark clouds of the ecclesiastical conflict gathered above the Reformed (*Gereformeerd*) Churches in The Netherlands. For this question there is only one answer: Because the Lord had a calling for me also in regard to that sad conflict. Otherwise I would not have returned at *that moment* before the schism had taken place. At *that time* the Lord wanted to use me. If not, He would have left me in Dachau. What did He want to use me for? What was my new calling? It was for me to do my part in maintaining the unity of the Church. And that had to be done only in the way of truth and righteousness. For that cause I immediately got to work, though I have to admit that at first I had the inclination to withdraw myself from everything. Is it surprising that after all the misery I experienced, as well as all the riches of the communion with God, that I originally was appalled about the sad, and in my opinion unnecessary, conflict in the Reformed (*Gereformeerd*) Churches? But I had to obey my calling now that I had returned at this time. For that reason I wrote an appeal to Synod. Synod did not deem it worthy of a reply. My consistory approved a proposal of mine and sent that to Synod. It was a plea to keep the unity of the churches. The result was negative. *They cast the die in all respects.*

After that there was only one way left to seek and keep the unity of the Church. That way I went obediently, as I had promised, without looking to the right or to the left. And that way was *liberation* from the sinful decisions of the General Synod by throwing off of a yoke which was not the yoke Christ put on His Church.

The continuing liberation of the Church, and to work for that with all my strength and talents, was the calling which I had received from the Lord, by His grace and at that time, after I had been a spectacle to the world and to angels and to men.

May God make me faithful in this calling for the further glory of His Name.

Finally, I want to write a word of heartfelt gratitude to all who by their love, their sympathy, their suffering along with us, and especially by their prayers, in the unity of true faith have supported and strengthened me during my imprisonment. May it also be a comfort for them to know that also these "good works" will be remembered by God. For these things which they did for me, they actually did for Christ. In me He was hungry and in me He was in prison. That is why He said, "Assuredly, I say to you, inasmuch as you did it to one of the least of these My brethren, you did it to Me."

With heartfelt gratitude I also remember the many people, committees, and businesses who nourished me by sending packages of food which helped me to stay alive. Besides God, I owe my life to these beautiful institutions and helpers. What they did has often deeply moved me. I owe them all much, very much gratitude, and will never forget what they did. If I would name them all the list would be too long. I believe to act in their spirit by not mentioning any of their names. All of these names are known to God, and that is most important. May God's blessing rest on their helpfulness which was such a blessing to me.

The poem at the beginning of this book was written by the late Mrs. C.E.T. Luykenaar Francken-Schreuder shortly after I was imprisoned. With deep gratitude for this token of sympathy I felt I had to place it in the front of this book.

Schilder's Struggle for the Unity of the Church
by Rudolf Van Reest

Klaas Schilder is remembered both for his courageous stand in opposition to Nazism, which led to his imprisonment three months after the Nazis overran the Netherlands in 1940, and for his role in the Church struggle in the Netherlands, which culminated in 1944 with the suspension of scores of office-bearers and the formation of the liberated Reformed Churches.

Thomas Vanden Heuvel in *The Outlook*: I strongly recommend this book for everyone interested in the preservation of and propagation of the Reformed faith.

Time: 1890-1952   **Age: 16-99**
ISBN 0-921100-23-X   **Can.$29.95 U.S.$26.60**

Secession, Doleantie, and Union 1834 - 1892
by Hendrik Bouma

. . . Bouma the story-teller charms us with a moving story about ecumenicity's outward, public side. . . In good Dutch Reformed style, Rev. Bouma wants things out in the open.
— From the *Introduction* by Nelson D. Kloosterman

Subject: Church History   **Age: 14-99**
ISBN 0-921100-36-1   **Can.$15.95 U.S.$13.90**

The Practice of Political Spirituality
by McKendree R. Langley
Episodes from the public career of Abraham Kuyper, 1879-1918

"In an age in which Christians sense a growing warfare with secular humanism, McKendree R. Langley's thorough study of Abraham Kuyper's largely successful application of Christian political ideas to Dutch life is extraordinarily valuable."
— Joel Nederhood

Time: 1879-1918   **Age: 16-99**
ISBN 0-88815-070-9   **Can.$9.95 U.S.$8.90**

The Romance of Protestantism
by Deborah Alcock

The Romance of Protestantism addresses one of the most damaging and (historically) effective slanders against the Reformed faith, which is that it is cold and doctrinaire. What a delight to find a book which documents the true warmth of the Protestant soul. I recommend this book highly.
— Douglas Wilson, editor of *Credenda/Agenda*

Time: 1300-1700   **Age: 12-99**
ISBN 0-921100-88-4   **Can.$ 11.95 U.S.$ 9.90**